# THE
# COLONIAL
# EXPERIENCE
## 1607–1774

by
**Clarence B. Carson**

A Basic History of the United States
Volume One

# THE
# COLONIAL
# EXPERIENCE
# 1607-1774

by
**Clarence B. Carson**

American Textbook Committee
*www.americantextbookcommittee.com*

email Byron_Mallory@hotmail.com

Photographs in this book are reproduced from the collections of the Library of Congress

ISBN 1-931789-09-6

Dedicated
to the Memory of
**LAWRENCE P. MC DONALD, M.D., M.C.**
(1935-1983)
An American Hero

Lost at Sea in the Korean
Airlines Massacre by Soviet
Communist Fighter Planes

**Other Books**
**by**
**Clarence Carson**

The Fateful Turn
The American Tradition
The Flight from Reality
The War on the Poor
Throttling the Railroads
The Rebirth of Liberty
The World in the Grip of an Idea
Organized Against Whom? The Labor Union in America
The Colonial Experience
The Beginning of the Republic
The Sections and the Civil War
The Growth of America
The Welfare State
America: From Gridlock to Deadlock
A Teacher's Guide to A Basic History of the United States
Basic Economics
Basic Communism
Swimming Against the Tide

# Contents

## Prologue

# Why the Study of History?

It has sometimes occurred to me to ask for a show of hands by those in a beginning class in history of those who have heard the old saying, "Experience is the best teacher." Usually, most of those in a class will raise their hands. It was a trick question, for I had led them to acquiesce in a way of putting it that is probably a garbled version of a saying. What Benjamin Franklin had said, I then told them was, "Experience keeps a dear [that is, costly, expensive] school. The fool will learn in no other." Far from being the best teacher, as Franklin would have it, experience is a teacher whom the wise will consult as rarely as possible.

There is a sense, of course, in which experience may be the best teacher. There may even be a saying to that effect. If so, it means something like this: Personal experience is the most effective teacher. That is, first-hand experiences are often more vivid, leave a deeper and longer-lasting impression. So it is that we say, "The burnt dog dreads the fire." On the other hand, personal experience is hardly the recommended approach to learning much that we need to know. The dog may not survive his first contact with the fire. It is better not to learn about the dangers of a moving car by being run over by one. It would undoubtedly leave a strong impression, but, alas, it might be the last impression. Then, too, life is much too short for us to gain more than a smattering of knowledge by personal experience.

It follows, then, that Franklin's is much the wiser, broader, and deeper of the sayings. It follows, too, that one of the reasons for studying history is to broaden our knowledge much beyond what we could acquire from personal experience. The study of history is a way to learn in a much less expensive school. We can buttress our limited experience with the experience of the race, so to speak. Not that we ever achieve such an exalted goal, of course, but it is one of the purposes underlying the study of history.

Some distinctions may be helpful at this point. It is possible to distinguish between formal history, such as may be found in history books or be studied in the classroom, and informal history, such as is the possession of every person who has any sort of developed memory. To put it another way, we can distinguish between history that has been recorded, organized, polished, and stated, on the one hand, and that

1

which exists in the hodge-podge of private recollections that each of us has. In like manner, we can distinguish between folk sayings, such as those quoted above, and the conclusions which may flow from formal historical studies.

Let me emphasize, though, that all these things are history, or the results of history. Those who say that they do not like history probably mean that they do not like what they have encountered in the classroom or textbooks that goes by the name of history. They could hardly mean that they do not like history. Every story with some basis in fact is history. Every bit of gossip either purports to be or is history. All that has ever happened to a person is history. All our recollections of things past is history. Virtually every joke, every anecdote, every cartoon, every witty saying, and every clever portrayal of something is either history or draws its vitality from history. Even works of the imagination have some sort of grounding in history, else we would find it difficult to find any common ground for comprehending them. In short, anyone who truly did not like history would be hard put to find much, if anything, that he did like.

But why study history? Granted, that each of us is in one way or another full of history, that most, or all, that we encounter is in some sense historical, that is, has a history, why study it formally? One reason is to become aware of how much of what we are and do is history related. Another, as already noted, is to expand our own limited experience. Yet another is to bring our experience and that of others to consciousness so that we can use it more effectively. Even our own raw experience, gossip, and folk tales need organization and critical examination, such as can be learned in formal history, before we can make the best use of them. History brings us not only much additional information, but also sheds new light continually on what we already knew.

These and other reasons for studying history may be brought into focus by an aspect of a single historical question. When settlers came to the New World from Europe in the 16th and 17th centuries, they came in contact with people already living here. Although the European settlers were greatly outnumbered at first, they usually either conquered or drove or moved them out shortly. One of the questions this raises is why the Europeans won so generally in the conflicts which took place between them and the Indians. Several reasons can be advanced, but at this point I want to offer only one—one, it might be noted, that is not often listed. This particular explanation will apply most directly to the Indians which inhabited what is now the eastern coast of the United States.

The reason I want to suggest is that the Europeans were vastly superior to the Indians in their sense and knowledge of history. For example, William Bradford, who was a leader in the Plymouth settlement in

Massachusetts, conceived and wrote a book called, *Of Plymouth Plantation*, 1620-1647. No Indian at the time could have written such a book. In the first place, none could have done so, because the Indians had no written language. (The hieroglyphics of Central American Indians might have resembled writing, but evidence that anything like an alphabet had been devised is lacking.) In the second place, Bradford's vision of the importance of the events would have been missing. And, third, the practice of preserving records did not exist among the East Coast Indians.

The matter goes much deeper than that, however. The Indians had only a shallow, provincial, and vague sense of history, at best. The alterations in the moon, the recurrence of the seasons, and such like, were familiar, of course. But their dating of things was imprecise, and their memories largely confined to that of living persons. By contrast, the European settlers had written records, history books, calendars, and the means for preserving precise information. Europeans with any formal training or learning, and many did, had a sense of history going back for thousands of years. They had the Bible and knew of the Hebrew prophets who spoke and wrote of people and events that went back to a time when there was a thriving civilization in Egypt, well before Greece and Rome emerged. They knew of Greece and Rome, and some could read Latin and Greek. They had in their minds such momentous religious events as the Creation, the Egyptian Bondage, the Diaspora, the Incarnation, the Resurrection, and looked forward in time to the Final Judgment. Men of learning knew of other religions such as Islam, and might even be acquainted with its history. Of modern history, they were most apt to be acquainted with the leaders, ideas, and events surrounding the Protestant Reformation. Before the Pilgrims landed at Plymouth William Shakespeare had written his great tragedies based on historical characters from Roman times to the Middle Ages, to what were for them, recent times. A good case can be made that the sense of history was especially strong at the time that Englishmen made the first settlements in America.

Their sense and knowledge of history provided the European settlers with an edge over the Indians. It endued them with an awareness of their place in the scheme of things. It gave vitality to their belief that they had a special purpose, a mission, and even a destiny. The fullness of their awareness of the past gave vitality to their vision for the future. When they could, Englishmen built houses of stone or brick. These contrasted dramatically with the scant dwellings of the Indians. The first were built to withstand many of the ravages of time; the second could survive, at most, a few seasons. The Indians were no match over any extended period of time for Europeans who brought so much of history to their undertaking.

It is not my point, of course, that the study of history will make us invincible in battle or will enable us to overcome those who have not studied deeply in history. Rather, my point is that the study of history adds an important dimension to our lives. It fortifies us for life itself with the knowledge of the path others have taken. If it falls to our lot to be soldiers, we may indeed be better soldiers if our experience is buttressed by a knowledge of the courage that others have shown in similar situations, by some acquaintance with what has failed or succeeded in the past, by the familiarity we have gained with what moves men to behave in certain ways. But whether we are soldiers, statesmen, businessmen, farmers, employers, employees, butchers, bakers, or candlestick makers, the study of history will enrich us for the undertaking.

One of the ways that history enriches is that it is the story of actual people, actual events, and some sort of actuality in the past. History is concrete, not abstract. There was a man by the name of Herodotus who lived in Greece (Athens) in the fifth century before Christ. He wrote history, and some of his work still survives. The Punic Wars did actually occur in the third century B.C. There was a Roman ruler called Augustus Caesar who was head of the vast Roman Empire at the time that Jesus of Nazareth was born. There was a man called Abelard, a monk who taught at Paris in the 12th century A.D., who was a popular teacher, drew many students to that center of learning, wrote a book titled *Yes and No*, and who fell in love with a nun, whose name was Heloise. William of Normandy did indeed complete his conquest of England at the Battle of Hastings in 1066. A kind of census (the *Domesday Books*) was taken shortly after the conquest, and much of the information about the England of those times comes from it. Hundreds and thousands of additional examples could be given, but perhaps the point has been made, at least tentatively. History is an account of things that actually happened.

It has been said that "History is philosophy teaching by example." No, that will not do, for we are dealing with the factuality of history, and a vague statement about its origin will not do. Lord Henry St. John Bolingbroke (1678-1751), an English statesman and writer, said, "History is philosophy teaching by example." I have it on the authority of Professor Henry Steele Commager, from the little book, *The Study of History*, that Bolingbroke was the coiner of the statement. If I had any reason to doubt this, I could trace it to other sources, including the writings of Bolingbroke. This little excursion was appropriate, because students sometimes wonder how we know all that we assert to have happened in history. My point is that a great deal of trouble has been taken to prove the correctness of many alleged facts, and, in many instances, the evidence is still available for any who would make the effort to verify their accuracy. That is not to say that every statement which appears in a history book is indeed factual. There are errors, well-known ones in some instances, that have been repeated from one book to another. They are corrected from time to time. But the very fact that we can identify errors is testimony to the factual character of history.

Now back to the matter of history being philosophy teaching by example. It might be more precise to say that history is general truth teaching by particular instances. But however the thought should be worded, it certainly is an aspect of history. For example, Lord Acton said, "Power tends to corrupt, and absolute power corrupts absolutely." If the statement is correct, it is a general truth. Does history provide examples of the truth of this axiom? Unhappily, it does, and many times over. History provides numerous examples of people who became vicious, cruel, avaricious, bloodthirsty, and so on, and it can be shown all too often that they possessed power over others. Infamous examples of absolute power corrupting absolutely are Caligula in Ancient Rome, Ivan the Terrible in Russia, Henry VIII of England, and, in the 20th century, Adolf Hitler and Joseph Stalin. A good example of the tendency of power to corrupt occurs in the account of David and Bathsheba in the *Bible*. King David saw Bathsheba and desired her. Bathsheba was married, but David sent her husband into battle where he was killed. Then, David seduced Bathsheba.

Its factuality is essential to this philosophical use of history. The evil rulers mentioned above are not fiction, are not inventions of the imagination, not simply the tales of moralists. They actually lived and did many, most, or all of the deeds reported of them. Thus, history brings to life the truth of axioms, of principles, and of great enduring truths. In short, there are great lessons to be learned from the study of history. History provides continuous examples for the good and bad consequences of acts. Careful students of history discover pitfalls to avoid as well as courses of action which promise good and desirable results. Above all, history reinforces with live examples what we may have learned first from other sources.

There are many other ways than by learning or having examplary lessons reinforced by the study of history to be enriched. It is mainly by the study of history that we learn how things in the past were different from or similar to the way they are today. An historian of the Middle Ages, Frederick B. Artz, once observed in a lecture that historians ought to teach classes about changes on Monday, Wednesday, and Friday, and about what does not change on Tuesday, Thursday, and Saturday. An attitude, particularly among the young, that cropped up in the 1960s illustrated well the need for this. It was the notion that those over 30 were not worth listening to because they could not be trusted. Although it was hardly the first time in history that youth has defied age, it was one of the more dramatic episodes of it.

History provides invaluable information both about the changing and the enduring. One of the pleasures that may come from the study of history, of course, is to learn how peoples at other times and places differ from us. We may be amused by the quaintness of their expressions, the strangeness of their dress, the odd (to us) notions they had about how to do things, the peculiarity of their customs, and so on. Yet, if we look closer, we will discover that in many fundamental ways they were hardly different from us at all. They laughed and cried, married and gave in marriage, loved and hated, bled when cut, resented slights, had preferences and fears, and much else besides. Power corrupted in ancient Egypt as it does in contemporary Russia. Even the young may have had pretensions to being wiser than their elders, for all we know. On reflection, we may conclude that in the most obvious ways that we differ from people at other times it is only a matter of fads, fashions, matters of no great consequence. There are differences that matter, of course, changes that have great importance, but to discern those from fads and follies, history can be quite helpful.

There is much else to history, of course. There is the pleasure of reading a good story. Some accounts of certain happenings in history can be told as the unraveling of a mystery. It may be possible to do biography as character development or disintegration, as in a novel. There are daring deeds, tense encounters, dastardly skullduggery, and stirring romances in the pages of history. There can be, too, the pleasures of visiting quaint and exotic places. Hundreds and thousands of places have the potential charm in history that we encounter when we visit the restoration of Colonial Williamsburg.

There may be no better way, however, to become aware of the importance of studying history than to imagine ourselves without it. Here is an apt description of that condition, as imagined by an historian writing early in this century:

> *Suppose that all knowledge of the gradual steps of civilization, of the slow process of perfecting the arts of life and the natural sciences, were blotted out; suppose all memory of the efforts and struggles of earlier generations, and of the deeds of great men, were gone; all the landmarks of history; all that has distinguished each country, race, or city in past times from others; all notion of what man has done or could do; of his many failures, of his successes, of his hopes; suppose for a moment all the books, all the traditions, all the buildings of past ages to vanish off the face of the earth, and with them the institutions of society, all political forms, all principles of politics, all systems of thought, all daily customs, all familiar arts; suppose the most deep-rooted and sacred of all our institutions gone; suppose that the family and*

*home, property and justice were strange ideas without meaning; that all the customs which surround each of us from birth to death were blotted out; suppose a race of men whose minds, by a paralytic stroke of fate, had suddenly been deadened to every recollection, to whom the whole world was new. Can we imagine a condition of such utter helplessness, confusion, and misery?*[1]

To remedy this natural state of things is why the study of history.

# Chapter 1

# Introduction

There was no United States prior to July of 1776. Indeed, there is good reason to doubt that there was a United States of America that early. True, the Declaration of Independence, which was signed on July 4, 1776, does contain the phrase, "the united States of America." But that was not so much to name the union as to distinguish between the former status of colony and the new status of state, once independence had been declared. Note, too, that the "u" is not capitalized, which suggests that "united" was merely descriptive, not part of a proper noun.

The Articles of Confederation was the first document to prescribe the title formally. It says, "The Stile of this confederacy shall be 'The United States of America.'" Although the Articles were submitted to the Second Continental Congress in July of 1776, Congress did not approve them until November 15, 1777, and they were not ratified until March 1, 1781. Technically, then, there was no United States of America until 1781. It could be argued, then, that the history of the United States began in 1781, and that it would be appropriate to begin an account of it on that date.

To do so, however, would be to defy custom, ignore the general practice, and act contrary to common sense. The history of the United States no more began in 1781 than the life of a man begins, say, when he is elected as President of the United States. Just where an account of it should begin may be open to disagreement and even debate, but that it should begin before 1781 can hardly be seriously disputed. A case could even be made that the history of the United States should begin with the appearance of man on earth. However plausible this might be, it would be impossible to do so literally and impractical to tell any considerable portion of what is known. In practice, most American history books begin with the first English settlements in the New World, preceded by the background of the Europeans who came and the Indians who were here. That will be the approach here.

The importance of the European background for explaining the United States can hardly be exaggerated. The United States derives from and is an extension of Western Civilization. The center of that civilization has long been Western Europe, and it actually spread from the Mediterranean countries westward at an earlier time. The great developments in Western Europe in the two centuries or so before the English settlements are equally important. The United States can only be understood in terms of such developments as the Renaissance and Protestant Reformation which preceded it. These things can be told only in summary fashion here, yet enough must be put into the record to make the connections clear.

It is a commonplace that the United States is a land of immigrants. So far as it goes, the statement is quite accurate. In wave after wave, the immigrants have come: English and Scots-Irish, Dutch and Scots, Irish and German, Italians and Poles, Blacks and Chinese, Jews and Czechs, Cubans and Puerto Ricans. But all waves of immigration did not come at the same time, and they have hardly been equal in influence upon shaping America. The waves of immigrants from the British Isles, and especially from England came first and in largest numbers initially, and their influence has been greatest. It is obvious in the predominance of the English language, but is there, too, in hundreds of other ways. The American Indians left their mark, too, even as they were vanquished, but, for good or ill, they played mainly an adversary role in the shaping of the United States.

The colonial period lasted for 169 years from the first English settlement in America to the Declaration of Independence. From that last event to the present, some 205 years have passed. That is a way of saying that the colonial period lasted a long time and encompassed the lives of something like eight generations of people. It will be of particular importance to us to note how things changed over the years, how population increased and spread inland, how they grew away from England, and, above all, how they gained experience which stood them in good stead when they broke from England and set up governments for themselves. Although it is well to reflect that they lived their lives for themselves primarily, even as we do, it is nonetheless true that we view them from a perspective of how they were preparing the way for and shaping institutions and ways of living with which we are familiar. The interpretations they made of their experience and the experiences they had influenced greatly what they did.

The colonial period, too, provides much useful information about how different America was then from now, how covered with forests it was, how remote in time the settlements were from one another, how difficult it was to travel from one place to another—and how perilous—, how often women died in giving birth to children, how many families were saddened by the untimely death of children, at what costs people and goods were brought from the old world to the new, and how different their attitudes and practices were from ours about crime and punishment. The history that follows begins the story of how we got from there to here as a people.

# Chapter 2
# European Background

*To the world when it was half a thousand years younger, the outlines of all things seemed more clearly marked than to us. The contrast between suffering and joy, between adversity and happiness, appeared more striking....*

*The contrast between silence and sound, darkness and light, like that between summer and winter, was more strongly marked than it is in our lives....*

*One sound rose ceaselessly above the noises of busy life and lifted all things unto a sphere of order and serenity: the sound of bells. The bells were in daily life like good spirits, which...now called upon the citizens to mourn and now to rejoice, now warned them of danger, now exhorted them to piety....*

—**J. Huizanga,** *The Waning of the Middle Ages*

## Chronology

1338-1453—Hundred Year's War between England and France.

1348—The Black Death in Europe.

1453—Fall of Constantinople to Ottoman Turks.

1454—Invention of the Printing Press.

1492—Columbus discovers America.

1494—Treaty of Tordesillas.

1497—John Cabot lands in North America.

1517—Martin Luther begins Protestant Reformation.

1519-1521—Magellan's ship sails around the World.

1536—Calvin publishes *Institutes of Christian Religion*.

1545-1563—Council of Trent (Catholic Reformation).

1588—Defeat of Spanish Armada.

1618-1648—Thirty-Year's War (Wars of Religion).

There are two distinct ways to look at what was happening in Europe in the century or so before Columbus discovered America. One way is to view what was going on in terms of what we now know was going to happen. Looked at in that way, in terms of the beginning of the Renaissance, of the coming Protestant Revolt, of the age of exploration that was just around the corner, it is possible to focus upon and find evidence that Europeans were preparing themselves for these great events. They were making inventions, discovering new possibilities, developing greater curiosity about the world beyond their knowledge, and trying to recover ancient learning. With the benefit of hindsight, we can tell the story that way, and, since that is a part of the story, we will return to it shortly.

Another way to look at the 14th and 15th centuries in Europe, however, is from the angle of what went before. From that angle, a major civilization was breaking up, declining, and losing its hold on a people. There had been a Medieval civilization. It reached its peak of organization and vitality in the 12th and 13th centuries. Signs that it was waning began to appear in the 14th century, and by the late 15th century what remained were largely relics and remains of a once great civilization. Thus, it will be necessary to understand a little about the Middle Ages in order to understand what was going on in Europe at the time of the discovery of America.

Before doing so, however, there are two concepts that need clarification. One is the concept of civilization. Although civilization may be defined in different ways by different writers, and historians sometimes differ as to how they are to be classified, there is one point on which there is general agreement. Civilization is an advanced condition of human arrangements and achievements. One dictionary defines it as "An advanced state of human society, in which a high level of art, science, religion, and government have been reached." Civilization can also be thought of in terms of the conditions which make such an advanced state possible. Peace and order must be established over a considerable area. All the peoples within a civilization do not have to be under a single government, but they must have common and agreed upon means for settling disputes and interacting peacefully with one another. There must be an economic base for it, extensive trade, and some division of labor, else people will not be freed from the business of getting a living for other pursuits. Indeed, civilization, as a concept, is closely related to the city. One word, "city," derives from the Greek word, *civitas*, which is the root also of "civilization." That is no accident, for there has never been a high civilization without cities.

The other concept is that of the rise and fall of civilizations. That civilizations have risen and fallen is as certain as that there were once civilizations, the Minoan for example, that no longer exist. But the concept has greater significance than that may suggest. In the past couple of centuries the notion has taken hold that man makes progress on a straight line upward. There is little place for such a belief in the fact of the rise and fall of civilizations. There is a kind of progress upward, though not in a straight line (there are bends and crooks) in technology, that is, in techniques for doing things and tools. But in the ability to maintain order, in the establishment of peace, in thought, in the arts, in economic arrangements, in most of those things associated with civilization, there is no clear line of upward progress in recorded times. No people is ever more than a generation, a generation untaught in the arts of civility, that is, away from barbarism. So far as can be told from the record of history, we are always nearer to the edge of the abyss of decay, decline, and disintegration than it is easy to imagine in peaceful and orderly times.

## The Classical Heritage

The Middle Ages was largely a compound of Classical, Christian, and Germanic elements. Since the Classical was first in time, it will be taken up first. What is referred to as the Classical culture took shape in Greece (6th to 4th century B.C.), was spread around the Mediterranean and is known as Hellenistic Civilization (4th to 2nd century B.C.), and took on a Roman cast in the Roman Empire, which was at its peak from 1st century B.C. through the 4th century A.D. Not only did the Classical Age make a great impact on the Middle Ages but also upon modern Europe and, eventually, upon the United States. It is most doubtful that there would have been a United States government such as was provided for in our Constitution had there not been the example of ancient Rome. The very idea of a republic came to the Americans from Rome. Both the word "Senate," and the idea was Roman. The idea of a mixed government, such as ours, was formulated in the Classical Age. Both the idea of democracy and the distrust of it comes to us from Greece. Many of the men who were leaders in making the United States Constitution were deeply studied in ancient history. And that is only to touch the political side of the Classical heritage.

Athens was the leading city during the Golden Age of Greece. For a century or so, a remarkable civilization flourished at Athens and surrounding cities. In the 5th and 4th centuries B.C., when Rome was little more than a primitive village, when Northwestern Europe was occupied by savage tribes, when the islands separated from Europe by what we call the English Channel were not yet named Britain (and over 1,000 years before there was an England), civilization was reaching a new peak in Greece. There was an outpouring of literary and artistic invention such as had never occurred anywhere before. Plato gave definite shape to speculative philosophy. Indeed, it has been said that all of philosophy since is a series of footnotes to Plato. Aristotle, his pupil, gave the scientific cast to philosophy. Herodotus is usually described as the "Father of History." Thucydides may well have been the first critical historian. Hippocrates, about whom little that is definite is known, can be thought of as one of the founders of scientific medicine. Sophocles and Aristophanes were great playwrights. Greek architecture, well exemplified by the Parthenon, demonstrates to the eye the classical idea of balance, proportion, and harmony. Greek statues were equally impressive examples of these ideas.

Probably, the most important contribution of the Greek Golden Age to all who participate in their heritage is the idea that there is an order underlying all things in this world. It is not an order made by man, but it is an order for man and for all things. The Greeks were not the first people to glimpse that order, of course. Men have long observed that there are regularities in nature, and they knew of many of these before the Golden Age of Greece. Those who lived near the seas perceived the regularity of the coming in and going out of the tides. All who will stare up into the heavens may glimpse the order in the regular phases of the moon. The seasons of the year follow one another in predictable fashion, and, having completed their cycle, they recur. Seeds taken from a plant reproduce that plant, other things being equal. Animals go through a cycle of life: birth, growth, maturity, death.

But the greatest of the Greek thinkers widened and greatly extended this idea of regularity and order. They sought to find an explanation for it. Above all, however, is that they attempted to universalize this conception, to extend into every realm. They perceived the underlying order as basically a natural order, and their approach to it was scientific, if that be understood as an attitude toward truth and not as a method. Aristotle was much closer to being what we would call a scientist than most thinkers of his time, but the cast of the thought of many others was scientific as well.

The Greek thinkers were fascinated with order, with regularity, with forms, with essences, with that which is not seen, nor felt, nor heard, but yet gives its character to all things. The great realities, Plato held, were the True, the Beautiful, the Good, and the Just. With their minds they were reaching toward things which were everywhere true. This set them apart from other peoples in their time and set the stage for political, legal, economic, and religious developments which followed in the ancient Mediterranean world.

The Greeks during the Golden Age were at heart provincial people. They were organized into city states, each separate and distinct from the other. Their religion, their commerce, their ways of life were so tied up with their particular cities that they could not conceive of, or want, a political organization that would unite all the Greeks. The nearest they could come to this were leagues or confederations, and jealousies among them usually tore these apart. While their greatest thinkers were beginning to think in universal terms, their city states remained the central focus of their lives.

The failure of the Greeks to conceive or set up effective broader political organization, plus the debilitating wars between and among the city states, set the stage for their conquest in the 4th century. Philip of Macedon (an outlying barbarian state, as the other Greeks thought of it) conquered the whole peninsula. His son, Alexander (the Great), proceeded to the conquest and formation of a vast empire surrounding the eastern Mediterranean. Aristotle had taught Alexander, and it may be that he learned from that great teacher something of the meaning of the quest for universal truth. But if he did, he applied it by force rather than persuasion and conversion, for he founded an empire to be ruled by despots. Alexander died (323 B.C.) shortly after completing his conquest. Within a few years of his death, the empire he had forged fell under regional rulers.

In the wake of the imperial conquests of Alexander, Hellenistic Civilization spread around the Mediterranean. Indeed, as a result of the conquest, West and East were brought closer together, and both Greek and Oriental ideas gained sway. The civilization that flowered and that was still dominant over much of the area down to and through the time that Jesus lived (4 B.C. to 29 A.D., the dates that have been widely accepted) was Hellenistic. That is, Greek influence was prominent, if not dominant. Nor did it end with the Roman conquest of the Greeks. The superiority of Greek thought to that of the Romans made its impact upon Rome, even when the teachers were slaves and the students were conquerors.

The most important contribution of Rome to civilization, aside from the Roman Catholic Church, was law. Roman imperial organization, Roman roads, aqueducts, architecture, and the Senate were remarkable achievements, but the accomplishments in legal development outshone them. The Romans discovered a way to govern not only those who shared with them a common culture but also peoples of diverse cultures and experiences. They ruled not only Romans but also Greeks, Persians, Jews, Egyptians, Spaniards, Britons, Franks, and those of many other lands. And they did so keeping basic justice as their goal.

The law by which the Romans ruled over diverse peoples was called the "law of nations" sometimes. That is somewhat confusing, because it sounds as if it would refer to the laws in operation in particular nations. On the contrary, it was the law that applied to all nations or peoples, the natural law, as it came to be called. The Stoic philosophers developed the conception of natural law much beyond anything the earlier Greeks had conceived, and Cicero brought the conception to the peak of its clarity. This law is discovered by reasoning on the nature of

## Marcus Tullius Cicero (106-43 B.C.)

Cicero was the great orator and philosopher of the Roman Republic. He was trained as a lawyer, learned in Greek philosophy, spokesman for the natural law philosophy, defender of the Roman constitution and the Republic when these were losing ground before the onslaught of despots who were busily building an empire. It is not surprising, then, that he was murdered by the despots. Cicero was, for the Founders of the American Republic, the great statesman of Rome.

things, he said. " 'For law,' " Cicero said, quoting from learned men, " 'is the highest reason implanted in nature, which prescribes those things which ought to be done, and forbids the contrary.' And when this same reason is confirmed and established in men's minds, it is then law." The Romans also conceived of constitutional law, which, for them, was found initially in the Twelve Tables of the Law. They also developed extensively their own civil law as well.

Basically, though, the Romans were conquerors. They were law givers, too, but this served more to enable them to rule than to maintain peace. There were periods, of course, during the centuries-long reign of Rome when peace generally prevailed over the vast domain. That accomplishment was never quite forgotten during the darkest of the Dark Ages, and the dream of restoring the Roman Empire in the West surfaced again and again during the Middle Ages. Indeed, a portion, at least, of the eastern empire survived throughout the Middle Ages. The Roman Emperor Constantine moved the capital to the east in the 4th century A.D., and it became known as Constantinople. The empire is known as the Byzantine Empire.

# The Christian Heritage

Long before that, however, momentous events had taken place within the bounds of the Roman Empire. God had revealed himself to man through the life and teachings of Jesus of Nazareth, who is known to all Christians as the Christ. Before exploring some of the importance of this for history, however, some background to this is in order. Christianity is a religion of the book. The book, of course, is the *Bible*. Among the major religions of the world, there is only one other that is a religion of the book—Islam. The *Koran* is the book of Islam. It is hardly an accident, however, that Islam (or Mohammedanism) came several centuries after Christ, or that it accepts Jesus and the Hebrew prophets as true prophets. That is, the *Bible* provided the example for the *Koran*. The two other cases in which there are sacred scriptures making up a book are too closely related to Christianity to be treated as separate instances. The Hebrew religion is also a religion of the book —the *Old Testament*, but that has been incorporated in the Bible. The Latter Day Saints have the *Book of the Mormon*, but they also accept the Bible and Christianity.

Since Christianity is a religion of the book, the written word assumes a special importance for Christians. Learning assumes a special importance. Careful construction of the meaning of words assumes a special importance. The original meaning, the original documents, the earliest applications, all assume a special importance. This is so especially for the scriptures, but the attitude and belief tend to be extended to more worldly books, documents, and words as well. While this attitude is true for all Christians, it is even stronger for Protestants than for others, and they set the religious tone for the United States.

The Christian heritage is often referred to as the Judeo-Christian heritage. It is appropriate that it should be. The Bible is a record not only of the beginnings of Christianity but also of the Jewish religion to that point. Much that Christians claim for their own, as well as do the Jews, is found in the *Old Testament*: The story of the Creation, the Fall, the Ten Commandments, the incomparable Psalms, the marvelous struggles of the followers of Yahweh (Jehovah, God), the reigns of David and Solomon, the Prophets, such as Jeremiah and Isaiah, and so on. The Jews reached a new level of religion with their belief in monotheism, that there is but one God, and that He is the great God Jehovah. That God is Just was an equally important concept. Most peoples in the ancient world believed in gods, but they were usually capricious gods for whom man was a plaything. Not so, the God of the Hebrews; he was a just God, wanting for man only what was for his ultimate good.

Looked at in the way of the world, the simple life story of Jesus does not belong in history books. History has to do with the great and the mighty, with conquerors and conquests, with politicians with hundreds of thousands of followers, with diplomats who drew up great treaties, with people of wealth, of learning, and of a vast influence on their contemporaries.

Jesus of Nazareth, the Christ, was none of these things. Of the things of the world, He had none of any consequence. It is written that the Son of Man had no place to lay his head. He was born in a stable, in a trough from which the animals ate. His parents were people of low estate. He must have had very little of formal education or training.

Legend has it that when He reached an age to work and provide for Himself, He learned and practiced the trade of carpentry. No organization ever set its seal of approval upon Him. On one occasion, Jesus noted that He was without honor even in his own town. He became what we would call an itinerant preacher, traveling here and there, addressing such audiences as would gather, usually outdoors, to hear him teaching and healing. In his wanderings, He gathered about him twelve men, men of ordinary pursuits mostly, whom we call his disciples.

True, considerable crowds gathered from time to time to hear. Many clamored for his attention, and one person even sought to get near enough to Him to touch his garments. But people of wealth and influence usually avoided Him. The rich young man turned away from Him sorrowfully, and people of prestige, if they came at all, usually came in secret, as Nicodemus did. Of all those things which a person is supposed to have, He had very little. The religious leaders suspected him of sedition. The Sanhedrin, a Jewish court, condemned Him and turned Him over to the civil authorities of Rome to be punished. He was condemned by a throng of accusers and, though Pontius Pilate, the judge for Rome, found no fault in Him, He was condemned to be crucified to please the crowd. At the last, the authorities offered to release Him, or such as the crowd might choose. They chose a notorious thief instead. As the world views such things, his origins were clouded, his life undistinguished, and his death ignoble.

That is surely not the stuff of history, and if the bare facts of his life were the whole story, Jesus would never have made his way into its pages. But there was more to the story, and much more to come. Jesus was born into a world in which there was a great longing for universality. And He brought a universal message. He taught that God is the universal Father, that He is a spirit, that He is unbounded love, and that He yearns to be at one, to atone, for men. He revealed by his life that there is a better way than the use of force, that there is a better way than military conquest. It is the way of love, of service, of persuasion, of influence, of kindliness, and of sacrifice. It is the way of life, He said.

Jesus Christ taught in words that have rung with great appeal down through the centuries. He spoke as never man had spoken, it was said at the time. For example, there are these words from the Sermon on the Mount:

Blessed are the poor in spirit; for theirs is the kingdom of heaven.
Blessed are they that mourn; for they shall be comforted.
Blessed are the meek; for they shall inherit the earth.

Blessed are they which do hunger and thirst after righteousness; for they shall be filled.

Blessed are the merciful; for they shall obtain mercy.

Blessed are the pure in heart; for they shall see God.

Blessed are the peacemakers; for they shall be called the children of God.

Blessed are they which are persecuted for righteousness sake; for theirs is the kingdom of heaven.

There is one crucial fact that was left out in telling the life of Jesus. The crucifixion was not the end. Jesus of Nazareth was put to death at the place called Golgotha, but Christ arose from the dead. The might of Rome, the greatest empire that had ever been, was unable to silence Him. Love bested force, and Sacrifice triumphed over the sword. Thus, the Revelation was completed.

One other point needs to be made before turning to the impact of Christianity on history. The point is that Christianity introduced a tension, or a set of tensions, into the affairs of men. The tension(s) takes many forms: the tension between man as he is and man as he should be, between this world and the next, between the sacred and the secular, between church and state, and so on. These tensions appear in every society in which there are any considerable number of Christians. (Since tension is one of the essential aspects of life, it should be noted that every society experiences tensions, as does every person.) There have been various efforts to resolve these tensions, and the attempts to do so are a part of history. In our day, there is an ongoing effort to radically separate the sacred and the secular and church and state. There are those who would have it that the sacred is personal and private and not a matter of social concern. They speak also of a wall of separation between church and state.

This attitude is profoundly at odds with Christianity, which is why it should be taken up before leaving the scriptural account. It is a reasonable interpretation of Scripture that God entered directly into the stream of human history through Jesus Christ. The Word was made flesh, Scripture says, and dwelt among us. The nature of the junction is a matter of doctrine on which sects and churches may differ, but that there was a junction which has never ended, is central to Christianity. Thus, the injunction traditionally used in marriage ceremonies seems appropriate here as well: "What God has joined together, let not man put asunder." To put the whole matter a different way, the sacred and the secular are woven together for Christians through Jesus Christ, and church and state are matters of Christian concern. That does not resolve the tensions, nor settle numerous questions that arise, nor is it intended to do so. It should explain, however, why both the sacred and secular are treated as appropriate subjects for history here.

Christianity spread rapidly around the Mediterranean during the remainder of the 1st century A.D. Paul, the Apostle, was one of the most active missionaries in this effort. He took on the task of being a missionary to the Gentiles and met with considerable success. Congregations and groups were founded in many communities. At first, the Roman Empire was a considerable asset in this undertaking. It provided order and safe passage over a vast region, plus good roads which made travel easier. The Caesars at first ignored or tolerated Christianity. Their attitude toward religion generally was, the more gods the merrier. And, if Christians had been willing to allow their God to become one among the Pantheon of gods, he would have been welcome to Rome. That was not possible, of course. By their Jewish religious heritage Christians knew that their God was a jealous God. He was not a god among gods, but the only true and living God. Nor could Christians accommodate themselves readily to emperor worship. Thus, they became a thorn in the flesh of Roman rulers and were subjected to persecution from time to time over the next 200 years. The persecutions did not succeed in wiping out Christianity, but they did tend to give that unity to it which arises from being a persecuted minority.

In the 4th century A.D., however, the fortunes of Christianity changed greatly. The Emperor Constantine proclaimed toleration for Christianity, and other religions, in 313. That he favored Christianity became obvious, however, when he called a council of bishops to settle questions of doctrine, had his children brought up as Christians, and was baptized himself at the time of his death. Later on in the century, Christianity became the recognized religion of the empire.

Actually, though, Christianity rose on the ruins of the Roman Empire. The Gothic (or German) invasions pressed more and more upon Rome, until a German was finally proclaimed emperor in 476 A.D. This is the traditional date for the end of the Roman Empire, or, at least, the western portion of it. Politically, Rome no longer ruled extensive lands. But the religious leadership of Rome was well on its way to being established. Bishops had for several centuries held religious authority over their particular regions or cities. Among the bishops, the Bishop of Rome asserted leadership, until the position began to be recognized as pope, or head of the Catholic church in the West. Gregory I, the Great (590-604), asserted the claims of the papacy so effectively that they were not soon challenged. The pope now occupied a place in religion analogous to the one the Caesers had formerly occupied politically.

# The Middle Ages

The learning and achievements of Greek and Roman civilization were very nearly forgotten in the early Middle Ages (6th through 10th centuries), also known as the Dark Ages. A lesser cause of this was the ambiguous attitude of Christians toward pagan culture. The learning of the Ancients was suspect because they were pagans, and Christians were fearful of being infected by it. Thus, they were less enthusiastic about preserving and continuing it than they might otherwise have been. On the other hand, such of Ancient learning and ways as were preserved during this period was largely by Christian scholars. It should be noted, too, that Rome was far gone in decay before it was overcome by invaders.

The main cause of the eclipse of civilization during this period, however, was the state of culture of the German invaders. By and large, the Germans were illiterate, pagan, farmers and warriors. As a rule, they neither understood nor cared about maintaining such of the Roman civilization as remained. For example, the Roman conquerors had built cities in Britain. When the German invaders came, they did not attempt to live in the cities. They would hardly have known how to keep them livable. Thus, they allowed them to decay and lived in the countryside instead.

Of course, Rome itself survived as did some other cities, and the rudiments of learning were preserved here and there, especially by the Church. But over much of western Europe a dark age descended. The slow missionary work of Christianizing the Germanic peoples was undertaken. Quite often, too, as soon as one wave of conquerors had been converted, a new wave of pagans from further north, or elsewhere, descended. Here and there, too, a revival of learning took place, schools were founded, and there was a reaching toward civilization, as during the rule of Charlemagne. But it was well into the 11th century before civilization on any scale began to appear again. In the 12th and 13th centuries Medieval civilization flourished and reached its peak.

Several aspects of this civilization need to be emphasized because of the heritage from it. It has already been noted that the three main ingredients in Medieval culture were classical, Christian and Germanic. The Germanic tended to prevail during the early Middle Ages, but it was increasingly modified by the classical and Christian heritages in the High Middle Ages. There was a revival of classical learning, spurred particularly by contacts with Moslem scholars in Spain. Great cathedrals were built, dominating the landscape of Europe. Many of these churches had schools associated with them. Universities were organized in many cities in Europe, such as Paris, Oxford, and Cambridge, universities which still exist in many cases.

Medieval society was organized into classes. Indeed, to understand class in the full dimensions as a legal condition, the place to study it is in the Middle Ages. There were three estates, or classes, in the typical arrangement. The first estate was the clergy; the second, the nobility; and the third, the serfs. According to the early formulation, the clergy prayed, the nobles fought, and the serfs worked. It was more complicated than that though. Each class had its own rights or duties, and differing laws which applied to it. For example, the priests had what was called "benefit of clergy." The phrase is still in use, but now it means that a person has been married. Then it meant something quite different. It meant that priests could be tried for offenses only in church courts. Each class or order had its own particular penalties for offenses, and, generally, the lower down in the class system an offender was, the stiffer the penalty. The system tended to be quite rigid, too, because except for the clergy, each person inherited the station of his parents. Like all true class systems, this system was imposed by law.

Everyone tended to be ranked in hierarchies in the Middle Ages. The clergy was ranked—pope to archbishop to bishop to archdeacon to deacon, and so forth—the nobility was ranked—emperor to king to duke to earl to knight, and so on—, and even serfs were ranked by function. In theory, every person must have an overlord, and this gave force to the ranks. If there was a belief in equality in the Middle Ages, it was thoroughly smothered.

The thrust of the Middle Ages was for everyone and everything to have its place, and for the whole to be brought into a single order. The Roman Catholic Church was the religious expression of this ideal. The Holy Roman Empire was as near as they ever got to the political realization of the ideal. The gothic cathedral, such as Notre Dame at Paris, was the visual expression of this ideal. The building began with its flying buttresses spread out on either side of the nave, with its spire reached upward to point toward the heavens. Art developed as decoration, mainly of churches, in the Middle Ages. Thus, painting was of stained glass windows, walls, and ceilings, and statues were fixtures on the buildings. Neither paintings nor statues had detailed individual features. Thus, persons were conceived as parts of a greater whole, rather than primarily as individuals. Dependency and interdependency rather than independence were the Medieval ideal.

The political practice of having a balance of powers may well have originated in the Middle Ages. The two great powers of the period were the Church, on the one hand, and the empire and kingdoms on the other. (The Holy Roman Empire never included all the kingdoms in western Europe.) Each had its own  powers or claimed its own powers, and they sometimes contested with one another for power. Power was further limited by the nobility, by high churchmen, and an assortment of lesser rulers. Almost every person of power was subject in some fashion to an overlord, and it was not uncommon for a noble to have several overlords.

One other point needs to be made about the Middle Ages at its peak. It was an age of the flowering of Christianity, an Age of Faith, Will Durant well said, an age when the spiritual wrestled for dominance over the minds of men as never before nor hardly since. That is not to say that people were better in that time than some other, that they kept the commandments more faithfully than at other times, or that a spirit of goodness generally prevailed. Hardly. Rather, it is to say that the religious motif was dominant, that church spires towered above all other buildings, that the most impressive architecture was religious, that art and thought were brought to the service of religion. The Church was vigorously reformed during this period, first by Cistercian monks, then by Dominicans and Franciscans. Francis of Assissi is the best known of the leaders of reform, but in many ways the most impressive of the reformers was Bernard of Clairvaux. His zeal extended into almost every realm; organizing monasteries, preaching crusades, putting dukes and kings in their places, and instructing the highest leaders of the Church. That the source of his strength was spiritual, however, none may doubt who read his moving words. Here, for example, is his vision of the rapture of the soul's union with God:

> O love, headlong, vehement, burning, impetuous, that canst think of nothing beyond thyself, detesting all else, despising all else, satisfied with thyself! Thou doest confound ranks, carest for no usage, knowest no measure....Everything which the soul-bride utters resounds of thee and nothing else; so has thou possessed her heart and tongue.

The Middle Ages reached its intellectual peak and culmination in the philosophy of Thomas Aquinas and the poetry of Dante. The "angelic Doctor," as St. Thomas came to be called, tried to harmonize all learning, ancient and Medieval, pagan and Christian, in his most ambitious work, *Summa Theologica*. His purpose was to bring all that was known into the service of Christianity. Dante wrote the *Divine Comedy*, which was a majestic effort to state in poetry the religious end toward which all things move, by writing of final things.

Signs of decline and decay began to appear in many directions in the 14th century and continued in the 15th. The Holy Roman Empire broke up into kingdoms, city-states, and independent cities. The idea of the empire remained, but it was much closer to fiction than to fact. The unity of western Christianity was shaken, even broken for a time, by events in the Church. In 1309, a French pope was elected. He took up his residence at Avignon, on the French border, and never went to Rome. A pope finally returned to Rome in 1376, but he died shortly thereafter. When a Roman pope was chosen to replace him, the French cardinals withdrew and elected their own pope, who took up residence at Avignon. There were two popes from 1378 to 1409; kingdoms and provinces gave their allegiance to one or the other of these, and Europe was religiously divided. When a new pope was elected in 1409, neither of the other two popes resigned, and there were, in effect, three popes. A great church council met at Constance in 1414 to settle the matter. Among those attending the council were 3 patriarchs, 29 cardinals, 33 archbishops, 150 bishops, 100 abbots, 300 doctors of theology, and 4,000 priests, among others. Although presumably they did not attend the meetings of the council, according to report, 1,500 prostitutes also assembled in the city. There can be little doubt that the Church had fallen on evil times. At any rate, the council deposed all those claiming to be pope and named one of its own choosing. The Great Schism in the church ended, but the decline of the hold of the Church upon Europeans continued.

The Black Death greatly reduced the population of Europe in the middle of the 14th century. Estimates are that from one-third to one-half of the population died over a two-year period. This greatly disturbed the social, political, and economic arrangements that had existed. There were attempts to fix wages where they had been, to freeze arrangements, as it were, but changes came anyway. The stable order of the Middle Ages had been greatly disrupted. It was further disrupted by the Hundred Years' War between France and England. The political affairs of the two countries had been intertwined since the Norman invasion of England (1066). At the end of this war they were disentangled.

One of the most obvious signs of decline was that the realm over which Christian rulers held sway was getting smaller. Far from being expansive, Christendom was receding. Crusades were no longer being launched to recapture the Holy Land. Constantinople fell to the Ottoman Turks in 1453. As H.G. Wells noted in his *Outline of History*, "A man of foresight surveying the world in the early sixteenth century might well have concluded that it was only a matter of a few generations before the whole world became Mongolian—and probably Moslem."

## *The Renaissance*

That was not to be, of course. Although the Moslems continued to press upon Europe for another century, Europe was already undergoing changes which would revitalize, reawaken, and send many peoples on an expansive course once more. Looked at from one angle, as noted before, the 14th and 15th centuries were a period of the decline and break-up of Medieval civilization. From another, it is the period when modern European civilization began to emerge. If we were transported back in time to 1500, say, we would undoubtedly be most impressed with how different from our times and strange to us almost everything was. We might even observe, probably rightly, that the times were much more like the Middle Ages than anything we would call modern. Yet modern changes in outlook from the Medieval to the modern had already taken place.

Since the Renaissance involved a change in outlook primarily, there are no events that can be definitely fastened upon which mark its beginning or end. It was clearly underway by 1450 and no longer the dominant mode by 1600. It developed first in Italy in the 15th century and spread vigorously into northern Europe in the late 15th and early 16th centuries. It flowered in dozens of directions: in an interest in ancient literature and learning, in voyages of discovery, in the development of national literatures written in the languages of particular countries, in art and architecture, in religious reformations, in scientific discoveries, and in a vast expansion of European trade and settlement activities.

What distinguished the Renaissance so clearly from the preceding age was a quickening of interest in life here on this earth, in the possibilities of the development of man along many lines, and in knowledge of the world about Europe. Men of the Renaissance did not so much rediscover the learning of ancient Greece and Rome as they did become aware of what a different world it had been. Thomas Aquinas had attempted to fit the Ancients within the Medieval framework; men of the Renaissance began the task of rediscovering them within their own time and place in history.

One of the important developments of the Renaissance was the going back to original manuscripts and documents. At the beginning of the 15th century, hardly anyone could be found in western Europe who could read ancient Greek. Even Greeks at the time spoke and wrote a language vastly different from that of the ancients. Two great interests were awakened by humanists—those interested in classical literature and learning. One was to recover old books and manuscripts. The other was to find those who could teach and to train people to read them. In 1396, a Greek named Chrysoloras was installed in the university at Florence in Italy. He taught Greek and inspired a vigorous search for old manuscripts. In the course of the 15th century numerous manuscripts were found in Constantinople and brought to Italy. The invention of the printing press around 1454 spurred not only the quest for books but also helped to spread them much more effectively and rapidly.

The importance of original languages and original manuscripts (or early ones) lies in the fact that languages change and decay with the passage of time. Later editions or copyings of works become corrupted from the original. Whether men of the Renaissance were impressed with this by their own discoveries, read Plato who was very conscious of this impact of the passage of time, or from some combinations of these with observation, they became very aware of it. The idea of going back to the original played an important role in the Protestant Reformation. It has always brooked large, too, in the attitude of Americans toward their Constitution.

Individuals emerged from the corporation—the orders and classes of the Middle Ages—in increasing numbers during the Renaissance. That is, individuals began to become independent, to stand on their own, to follow their own courses. The growth of trade and cities did much to foster this development. Cities and trade had become increasingly important in the High Middle Ages and probably contributed in their own way to the break-up. People who lived in towns and cities were often free (from serfdom or other feudal obligations) even in the Middle Ages. In the Renaissance, their independence was greatly enhanced. Some men acquired wealth and independence as tradesmen. But this individualistic trend occurred in many directions. Individual paintings made their appearance, as well as statues, separate from churches or buildings. Paintings, too, were frequently of individuals, showing their distinct features of face and body. Many gained fame and fortune, not as members of some group, but on their own.

Since the Renaissance tended to be individualistic, one of the best ways to see it, particularly in its aspect of promoting the development of a diversity of talents, is in the lives of individuals. Three men who illustrate the Renaissance outlook well are Cosimo de Medici, Leonardo da Vinci, and Erasmus. Cosimo's father had made considerable wealth in trade. Italian cities were centers of trade between East and West at the time. Cosimo de Medici was a citizen of Florence who devoted himself to business throughout his life and accumulated great wealth. He also gave much of his time to political activities, and, though he held no political office, eventually dominated the political life of Florence. Above all, though, he was a patron of humanistic learning and the arts. He learned Latin and Greek, and bought many manuscripts in both languages. He financed libraries, sponsored scholars, was a patron of painters, sculptors, and architects, provided a refuge for Greeks when they fled from the Turks, and built many fine structures. Not only does he illustrate the diversity of interests of a man of the Renaissance but also the close connection between trade, wealth, and the literary and artistic developments.

In no other single man was the diversity and genius of the man of the Renaissance so well exemplified as in Leonardo da Vinci. Although he was born in Florence, in the course of his long life he lived and worked in most of the great cities of Italy. He was a painter, sculptor, architect, musician, mechanic, engineer, inventor, and scientist. But even this listing cannot suggest the quality of work or the range of his achievements. He mastered new techniques in painting as well as painting such famous subjects as "The Last Supper" and "Mona Lisa." He worked more on the principles that would underlie inventing than upon inventions themselves. It is said that he knew already, a century more or less before them, what Galileo, Bacon, Newton, and Harvey would learn. Indeed, his scientific imagination outran scientific discovery and his ability to convey what he knew to others. His interests ranged from military engineering to color and lighting.

Erasmus was the most outstanding man of letters in the Northern Renaissance. By birth he was Dutch, but he lived his life changing from country to country in northern Europe. He became a monk and was ordained as a priest, but the discipline of such a life did not suit him. While he never left the Roman Catholic Church, he did manage to live much of the time outside its keeping. He found patrons, wrote, edited, and lived first here and then there, as opportunities presented themselves. Erasmus exemplifies well the spirit of the Northern Renaissance in which there was much greater religious emphasis than in Italy. He made a new translation of the *New Testament*, did many translations of the early church fathers, and wrote mainly on religious subjects. He believed that the Catholic Church had been corrupted by superstitious and unbiblical practices which had crept in over the years. The direction of his work and thought was to push toward a return to early Christianity. He did not, however, become a Protestant. Mostly, he remained on the sidelines in the contest between Protestant and Catholic leaders and repeatedly rejected Catholic leaders who tried to get him to throw his weight behind Catholicism.

One other point about the Renaissance needs to be made here. The word "humanism" is often used in connection with the Renaissance. Since the word has lately become a matter of controversy, particularly in the modified form of "secular humanism", some of its earlier uses need to be made clear. At the time of the Renaissance, a humanist was simply a person who studied and worked at recovering, translating and otherwise making available material from the ancient world. More particularly, some humanists also were much interested in the imaginative literature and arts of the ancient world. From this, humanism came to connote an interest in the human in contrast with a primary interest in the sacred or divine. This should not be taken to mean that humanists were anti-Christian, or even necessarily un-Christian. Some humanists were devout Christians, Erasmus, for example; some were conventional Christians, da Vinci, for example; and some may have been near-pagans in their ways of living, yet remaining nominally Christian. Humanism certainly did not imply atheism, as secular humanism does.

# The Protestant Reformation

The Protestant Reformation was both a product of the Renaissance and a profound rejection of much of its humanistic emphasis. The Renaissance certainly prepared the way for Protestants with its emphasis upon going back to early or original documents, upon corruption with the passage of time, upon exact translation, with its opposition to superstition, and with its critical attitude toward what had come down from the most recent past. Most Protestant reformers were themselves men of the Renaissance in background and training.

## Martin Luther
## (1483-1546)

Luther was first a monk, then a priest and a university professor as a Roman Catholic. He took positions contrary to those of his church in 1517. In consequence, he was found guilty of heresy, ordered to recant, and refused. After 1521, he became the leader of the Protestant Reformation in Germany, his native land, where he began to pick up support from local rulers. Luther translated the Bible into German and is the founder of the Lutheran Church.

On the other hand, if the Protestant Reformation was not an effort to restore the Medieval outlook it was at least an effort to revive the focus upon the enduring and the eternal, the concern with final things, above all, with salvation. The mysticism which was so prominent in the late Middle Ages was present among some of the reformers. The belief in witches and witchcraft, too, which had been widespread in the late Middle Ages continued to be widespread among Protestants. It certainly ran counter to the Renaissance outlook.

Most of the difficulties of providing exact dates for the Renaissance do not apply to the Reformation. Its beginning and spread can be dated with considerable precision. Martin Luther nailed his 95 theses (propositions) on the church door at Wittenberg in 1517. He was tried at the Diet of Worms in 1521 and commanded to recant (withdraw his opposition) on some of his positions. Luther declared that unless he was persuaded of his error by evidence from the Scriptures and reason he could not and would not recant. The Reformation was underway.

It spread rapidly, too, from place to place and country to country throughout northwestern Europe. Ulrich Zwingli succeeded in converting the German-speaking portion of Switzerland, or most of it, to the Protestant persuasion in the 1520s. Denmark became Lutheran in 1523, followed by Norway in 1537. England was taken out of the Roman Catholic Church in 1534, and in 1560 the Scottish church became Presbyterian.

All that is a way of saying, too, that Protestantism spread rapidly and that it must surely have been an idea for which the times were ripe. Certainly, there was a widespread belief that the Church needed extensive reform. Erasmus had done much to spread that idea. Renaissance popes lived in great splendor, lavished wealth upon fine furnishings for their residences, quite often had fathered several illegitimate children, and some were clearly depraved. The widespread sale and worship of relics (alleged remains of some part of the body of saints) was offensive to men of learning. The sale of indulgences (grants of forgiveness for sins) in order to raise money for great church enterprises was an open scandal. There had been no general reform of the Church for more than two centuries, and it had become increasingly a worldly institution. The Church resisted all efforts at reform, so that at last the only option left open for those who would have reform was to revolt from it.

The two most influential leaders of the revolt from the Roman Catholic Church were Martin Luther and John Calvin. Luther belonged to a strictly disciplined order of monks and was a teacher. By his own account, despite his blameless life according to the teaching of the Church, he was uncertain about his relationship to God. He was impressed by the majesty and goodness of God and did not see how as worthless a creature as man could merit salvation. The sacraments and other good works prescribed by the Church did not seem to him sufficient to bridge the gulf between him and God. Thinking this way, he says that it came as a revelation when he read the words in Romans, 1:15: "The just shall live by faith." And he came to believe that it was not through any efforts of his own nor by any good works that he could be reconciled to God. That was God's doing, not his. He had only to believe and accept.

Luther and his followers dispensed with most of the sacraments. Luther held that the individual must approach God through Jesus Christ, and that no human intermediary was either necessary or effective. Thus, much of the priestly function of the clergy was abandoned. In short, the Medieval forms of the Church were cut away. The swift spread of Protestantism suggests that in religion, as elsewhere, many people no longer felt or believed in the system that had prevailed. Note, too, that this direct approach to God was individualistic, not corporate. This did not mean, at the time, that the individual was free to choose his own church or ways of worship—that was something that would develop well into the future—, but it did mean that the individualizing tendency of the Renaissance was entering a new realm.

John Calvin was quite different in temperament, in training, and in the cast of his mind from Martin Luther. Calvin was French; Luther was German. That is difference enough in itself, though Luther may have increased the difference by his own influence. Luther translated the *Bible* into German, and this was certainly a formative influence on the German language. Luther was emotional, volatile, passionate, and somewhat erratic; Calvin was cool, rational, precise, and persistent. Luther was trained in the philosophy of the Middle Ages; Calvin was much more the scholar of the Renaissance. Above all, Calvin was trained in the law, and his theology was logical and legalistic. But their differences should not be overemphasized. Calvin claimed to be following in Luther's footsteps, to be developing his ideas, and accepting much he had done as correct. Their paths did diverge, however, in the churches that were founded. The Lutheran church derived from Luther. The Reformed churches, Presbyterian usually, derived from Calvin.

## John Calvin
## (1509-1564)

Although Calvin took training for the priesthood in the Roman Catholic Church, he turned instead to the study of the law. He broke from the Roman church in 1534 and was not long in emerging as the leading thinker in the Protestant movement. He left his native France in 1536 to take up residence in Geneva, Switzerland, where he spent most of the rest of his life. His interpretations of Christianity became the basis of the Reformed churches which were formed in many lands. American Puritanism and the Presbyterian churches were offshoots of Calvinism.

Calvin's most famous work was the *Institutes of the Christian Religion*. Protestant reformers generally placed great weight upon Scriptures, none more than Calvin. As one historian has said, "He saw the Bible as the sole reliable authority for our knowledge of God. Without attempting to accord equal weight to every passage of the Scriptures, he regarded the will of God as immutable and Christ as operating timelessly in both Testaments."[2] Calvin emphasized the sovereignty of

God, the evil nature of man, God's choice of men to salvation, and man's dependency on God. He set forth a series of doctrines, supported them with extensive scriptural references, and spelled out the logical implications of the beliefs. Calvin was the theologian of the Protestant movement, and his influence went much beyond those who accepted his specific beliefs as a whole.

As late as the 1560s, anyone following the course of religious developments in Europe might have concluded that all of the continent was going to be swept into the Protestant camp. The day of the Catholic Church was coming to a close, he might have concluded. Such an opinion would have been in error. At the very moment when it appeared that Catholicism was about to be overcome, the Church was headed for reform itself. At the Council of Trent, which concluded its business in the early 1560s, Catholic doctrine was reformulated and restated. The papacy had been reformed already. New religious orders, most notably the Jesuits, became the spearhead of a renewed religious zeal and vitality. Not only did the Church hold on to much of its following in southern Europe, but it became once again the church militant. Although Christian unity had been shattered, the vitality of Christianity had been revived in a diversity of churches.

# *The Rise of Nation-States*

What would become nation-states had already begun to emerge before the Protestant Reformation. Indeed, they had considerable to do. with the spread of the Reformation. Even so, it is appropriate to delay the discussion of the rise of nations to this point, for the process was brought to fruition by the Reformation.

The nation-state, or nation, is a modern development. In the ancient world and in the Middle Ages there had been city-states, kingdoms, and empires. Some of the ancient kingdoms might have been sufficiently independent that we could think of them as nations, but this was not so of Medieval kingdoms. The essential feature of the nation is that it is independent of other nations, that all power and authority exercised within its boundaries are contained within the nation. To put it another way, a nation is a realm in which no outside power has legal authority. The concept of the nation, in this sense, was alien to both thought and practice in the Middle Ages. The theory that every man should have an overlord ran contrary to it. Rule over realms was intertwined and entangled within the feudal system. For example, for much of the Middle Ages the king of England was a vassal of the king of France, at least for his French provinces. Local rulers in Germany and Italy were underlings to the Holy Roman Emperor. Moreover, the Roman Catholic Church, and especially the pope, exercised authority throughout western and central Europe. From time to time kings, and even emperors, acknowledged that they were vassals of the pope. This had to be swept away, or reduced to insignificance, for nation-states to develop.

In the late 15th century, three kingdoms—Spain, France, and England—were unified under a single rule and began to take on the appearance of nations. One other—Portugal—reached its present boundaries in 1463 and was early one of the most powerful nations of Europe. Until it was unified, Spain was a hodge-podge of small kingdoms, some of which were more Moslem than not. The first major step toward unification was the marriage of Ferdinand of Aragon and Isabella of Castile in 1469. This linked together in a single house the two largest of Spanish provinces. In 1492, the Moslems were driven out of Granada, and in 1512, Navarre was conquered. Thus, all of Spain had become a single kingdom.

France and England were disentangled at the end of the Hundred Year's war. However, the kingdom of France was still far from consolidated, since there were several major provinces not securely under the crown. Louis XI brought all the provinces, except Britanny, under his control in 1482-83. In 1491 the king married the duchess of Britanny, thus completing the consolidation of the kingdom.

In England the main difficulty was a dynastic quarrel between the houses of York and Lancaster as to which was the rightful heir to the throne. The result was the War of the Roses, which lasted from 1455 to 1485. In the end, Henry Tudor achieved the throne as Henry VII. Most of the nobility had been wiped out as a result of this fratricidal war, and Henry ruled without an effective opposition.

The emergence of nation-states provided the political framework for the spread of Protestantism. There should be no doubt that religious concerns were at the heart of the Reformation. It is likewise true, however, that it would not have spread so rapidly or been so quickly adopted in many lands if princes and kings had not adopted it. And their adoption of it was closely related to the desire to be rid of papal control of the church. Nowhere can this be seen more clearly than in England. Henry VIII took the Church of England out of the Roman Catholic fold, and he did so primarily to make the church his servant. The immediate issue was Henry's wish to divorce his wife, Catherine of Aragon, and marry Anne Boleyn. The pope denied his petition for a divorce, and he obtained one by making the church a national church. The English church was changed and reformed in consequence, but it was more in keeping with Renaissance than Protestant ideas of what needed to be done.

The princes and kings led the way in making the changes in Lutheran countries. The general rule for Lutherans was that the religion of the prince became the religion of his subjects. Thus, the Protestant Refor-

# Henry VIII
## (1491-1547)

Henry Tudor succeeded his father, Henry VII, to the throne of England and Ireland in 1509. He was imbued with the ideas and ideals of the Renaissance, though fate made him a man of the Reformation, and he has gone down in history as a womanizer. He established the Church of England by taking it out of the Roman church, beginning in 1529. However, he kept many of the Catholic forms and rituals, a Renaissance rather than Reformation performance. He did reform the church, however, joining him, somewhat tentatively to the Reformation. And, Henry married six women, sort of, though he may have been spurred more to this by the desire for a male heir than passion for the women. If he was a despotic king, he managed it within the framework of English law.

mation provided the opportunity for rulers to free themselves from Rome as well as the various allegiances that were supported by the Catholic Church. Reformed churches (Calvinist), on the other hand, depended much more on the conversion of church members to different beliefs. In any case, the Presbyterian method of control over the church did not lend itself especially well to the support of monarchy. There were sects, such as Baptists, Quakers, Moravians, born out of the Reformation which were not political in character. But wherever Protestants became dominant, the connection with Rome was broken, and the way was opened to the formation of nation-states.

However, France and Spain remained predominantly Catholic and also underwent the consolidation and centralization of power associated with nation-states. They were aided in this by the voluntary agreement by popes to curtail their powers in those kingdoms. Monarchs in Spain gained significant control over the Church in Spain when Pope Sixtus IV granted them the power to nominate church officials. In France, the kings actually appointed high church officials after 1516. This is one of the reasons that French kings were not much tempted to become Protestants.

The rise of nation-states increased the freedom and power of rulers but not of their subjects. It set the stage for absolute monarchy over much of Europe. The Medieval balance of power, to the extent that it had once prevailed, had been greatly reduced or virtually wiped out. Churches had little power any longer to restrain monarchs. In general, too, the consolidation of kingdoms was at the expense of the nobility, most of whom were reduced to courtiers of the monarch. Parliaments, which had grown more powerful during the late Middle Ages, lost much of their power, as, for example, the Estates General in France and the Cortes in Spain.

On the other hand, these consolidated kingdoms provided the push to the discoveries, explorations, and settlements in the New World. Spain, Portugal, and England were leaders, followed by France, Sweden, and the Netherlands. Neither Germany nor Italy played any significant role in the New World.

# The Age of Discovery

The era of the Renaissance was the great age of discovery of the rest of the world for Europeans. Indeed, so far as we know, no peoples had ever become aware of so much of the world before them. Before the 14th century only about 7 percent of the ocean surface and 21 percent of the land surface had been known. By 1600 something like 40 percent of the land surface had been explored and 52.5 percent of the oceans. But the greatest voyages of discovery were made in a period of less than 40 years, between the 1480s and 1521. After that, it was largely a matter of making the additional voyages and making the explorations.

Great journeys of discovery had been made from Europe before this time, of course. The Vikings had made voyages to America even some 500 years before the discoveries of Columbus. Marco Polo had traveled to far-off China two centuries before Vasco da Gama discovered a new sea route to Asia. He found a great empire ruled by the Great Khan, and for many years Polo traveled about that part of the world in the service of the emperor. He went mainly overland on his journey to China and returned mainly by sea. But the Viking voyages had almost no impact upon Europe, never became generally known, and America was hardly disturbed for long. Although Marco Polo's journeys received greater publicity, mainly because he wrote about them, Europeans were hardly in a position to act upon such information as he provided.

One way to explain the failure to use the knowledge acquired earlier is to say that the times were not right for it. Great voyages and journeys to the ends of the earth were barely repeatable flukes in the Middle Ages. Tales of America in 1000 A.D. might have been accepted as part of the lore people half believed, if everything there was vastly different from anything they knew. Marco Polo was suspected of inventing the land of Kublai Khan. True, there were those who accepted them, but the Arabs barred the overland route to the East, and no all-sea route was known.

At any rate, major changes and developments had occurred in Europe by the end of the 15th century. Renaissance activity spurred much greater interest in the physical world. The recovery of new aspects of ancient learning had not only awakened an interest in history but also in other places and peoples. Technical developments also opened up new possibilities. While the magnetic compass had been around for some time, the astrolabe, a device for determining latitude, only came into general use in the 15th century. Europeans were building bigger and better ships, and taking longer voyages generally at this time. Far flung trade gave impetus to shipbuilding. The consolidation of kingdoms provided the resources for discoveries and exploration. The printing press provided a means for much wider publicity for any discoveries. It is significant that within a few years of the discovery of America books began to appear about the New World.

There was much interest, too, in finding new trade routes to the East. The fall of Constantinople to the Turks did make trade more difficult, but it only hampered it. Wars with the Moslems who were pressing on Europe did pose threats to trade. But more than that, western European peoples were interested in breaking the Italian dominance of the trade with the East. Italian cities prospered greatly by this trade, for much of it came through their ports. By the late 15th century, many people from western Europe had seen the splendor of the Italian cities built on this trade. They wanted some of it for themselves.

The times may have been right for discoveries around the turn of the 15th century, but it was still bold, daring, and adventuresome men who made the discoveries, men such as Bartholomew Diaz, Christopher

## Christopher Columbus
## (circa 1446-1506)

Columbus was born in Genoa, Italy, and developed an early interest in the sea. As a young man, he fortified this interest with travels around Europe and the study of astronomy, geography, and mapmaking. The more he learned the more convinced he became that it would be possible to reach the Far East by sailing west. After many turndowns, he finally found a patron—Queen Isabella of Spain—for his enterprise. He made four voyages in all to the New World, and on one of these he discovered South America. Through his tenacity he had pointed the way to new continents, but they were named for another, and he died out of favor and without fortune.

Columbus, Vasco da Gama, John Cabot, and Ferdinand Magellan. The Portuguese took the early lead in voyages of discovery. This was largely the fruit of the efforts of the man known as Prince Henry the Navigator (d. 1460). His main interest was in exploring the west coast of Africa. Professor Wallace Ferguson suggests that his motives were mixed: "intellectual curiosity, the crusader's dream of outflanking the Moslem states of North Africa, the pious hope of bringing Christianity to the heathen, and a very practical desire to add to the territory and wealth of Portugal by discovering new areas for trade and colonization."[3] Prince Henry founded a school of navigation to realize his vision, and brought together mapmakers, students of geography, and navigators.

After Henry's death the work of actually exploring the coast line of Africa got under way. Portuguese sailors made longer and longer voyages. Finally, on an unusually long voyage, Bartholomew Diaz sailed around the Cape of Good Hope, confirming that he had located the southern tip of Africa. When that knowledge had been acquired, it was only a matter of time before voyages to China would be made by sea around Africa.

Before that happened, however, Christopher Columbus had discovered what we now know to have been islands in the Caribbean off the mainland of the Americas. Columbus was long on courage and short on knowledge. It was not simply that he did not know that the Americas existed, or that they lay across his path to Japan when he sailed west to reach the East. No one knew that. But Columbus was not familiar with, or did not accept, much that was known or believed by men of learning in his day. For one thing, contrary to the best estimates, he believed that the Asiatic continent was much wider than it is. For another, he apparently had no very clear idea of how far it is around the world. If there had been no land between the Canary Islands, say, and Japan he would have been at sea at least 10,000 miles, by the best estimates at the time. If such a voyage would not have been impossible, it would certainly have been improbable.

It is no wonder, then, that Columbus had difficulty finding a sponsor. He took his proposal first to the royal court in Portugal. When the experts pointed out the foolhardiness of his plan, the king turned him away. The experts were no more favorably disposed in Spain, where Columbus went next, but Queen Isabella nonetheless financed the voyage. He set sail from Spain August 3, 1492, and from the Canaries September 6. The winds were with him, as he had calculated, and he reached the islands off the Americas on October 12. He thought he had reached the Indies, as the Far East was called then, and he referred to the inhabitants he discovered as Indians. Columbus persisted in believing that he had found a way to Asia and made four voyages in a vain effort to discover the riches of the East. He failed in his effort to locate any wealth such as he sought, and he died in disgrace and poverty.

Columbus did not even receive the honor of having the lands he had discovered named for him. They were named instead for an obscure Florentine who had settled in Spain, Amerigo Vespucci. So far as is known, Vespucci may have made several voyages to the New World in the years immediately after Columbus. But it has never been established that he led any of them. However, several letters were written in his name. In one of them, Vespucci said: "These regions we may rightly call *Mundus Novus*, a New World, because our ancestors had no knowledge of them....I have found a continent more densely peopled and abounding in animals than our Europe or Asia or Africa." These letters were printed in Florence. The letters came to the attention of a German geographer, Martin Waldseemuller, who published a map of the world and gave as the name of the New World, America, after Amerigo Vespucci, whom he declared to be the discoverer. The name caught on within a few years. The power of the press was demonstrated at that early date.

Meanwhile, shortly after Columbus's first successful voyage, well before anyone was aware that a New World had been discovered, most of the non-Christian world was divided between Spain and Portugal. This was accomplished by the Treaty of Tordesillas in 1494. By its terms, Spain got the bulk of the New World, though, as luck would have it, Portugal got a claim to Brazil.

Even so, voyages of discovery and exploration got underway in earnest now. In 1497, John Cabot, sailing for the English king, discovered the east coast of North America. In 1498 Vasco da Gama, sailing for Portugal, finally found a sea route to the East. He sailed around the Cape of Good Hope, followed the African coast northward, and eventually made his way to India. The hope that a water passage through the Americas to the Far East lured explorers on once they became aware that a New World had been discovered. Balboa discovered that there was an ocean on the other side of America. But, of course, no such passage was ever discovered, for none existed. Finally, in the most daring voyage ever attempted, Ferdinand Magellan led a fleet which would sail around the world, 1519-1521. Magellan was killed in the Philippines, but the trip was completed by his crew. He not only confirmed the great distance between the Americas and Asia but also proved that more than Columbus dreamed could be done.

Although Columbus failed to win wealth and fame for his efforts during his lifetime, Spain, for whom he sailed, reaped rich benefits from his discoveries. Spain was the dominant power in the world for most of the 16th century. Spanish rulers not only ruled  as much  of the

## John Cabot
## (1450-1498)

Like Columbus, Cabot was born in Genoa, but he moved to Venice while still a boy. He, too, was taken with the idea of sailing westward to get to the riches of the East. It was this dream that prompted him to move to England in quest of a patron. Before he could accomplish anything, however, he heard of the voyage of Columbus, and this prompted him to undertake, for the king of England, a voyage in the same general direction. They reached islands off the coast of Canada in May 1497 and Cabot claimed the land for England. Although he made another voyage to the same area the next year, Cabot died before it became known that he had sailed to the New World, not Asia.

New World as they desired but also were the dominant powers in Europe. Charles V (Charles I in Spain) became king of Spain in 1518 and thereafter ruled Spain and much of central Europe for most of the next 40 years. Philip II, who succeeded him, ruled a vast domain, extending from the Netherlands to southern Italy to the Philippines to much of the New World. Great wealth was discovered in America, and most of it was hauled to the Old World in Spanish galleons. The Spanish fleet so completely dominated the seas for most of the century that other countries steered clear of the Americas.

# Chapter 3
# The English and America

*This royal throne of kings, this scepter'd isle,*
*This earth of majesty, this seat of Mars,*
*This other Eden, demi-paradise,*
*This fortress built by Nature for herself*
*Against infection and the hand of war,*
*This happy breed of men, this little world,*
*This precious stone set in the silver sea,*
*Which serves it in the office of a wall*
*Or as a moat defensive to a house,*
*This blessed plot, this earth, this realm, this England.*

—**William Shakespeare**

---

## Chronology

1485—Tudor Reign Begins.

1534—Church of England Established.

1560—Elizabeth I comes to the Throne.

1577-1580—Drake sails Around the World.

1585—Raleigh's Settlement on Roanoke Island.

1588—Defeat of the Spanish Armada.

1603—Stuart Reign Begins.

1606—Grant of Virginia Charter to London Company.

1611—Publication of King James Version of the Bible.

1620s—Suppression of Puritans.

1628—Petition of Right.

1642—Civil War in England.

1649—Charles I Executed.

1649-1660—Interregnum.

1660—Restoration of Monarchy.

Those who made the initial settlements in the eastern portion of North America that is now a part of the United States were not simply Europeans in origin. Most of them were Englishmen. By and large, too, they were proud of their English heritage and determined to preserve it. Even the changes they made from time to time were usually variations and alterations from the English model. It is well, then, to make some acquaintance with what Englishness meant at the time the settlements were made. But the settlers did not arrive upon an empty continent. There were people here already, those whom Columbus called Indians —and the name stuck. After all, Europeans were not the first discoverers of America; the Indians were. It is appropriate as well to take the Indians into account, and that will be done after some discussion of the English.

A major change in England's position in European civilization was occurring at the time of, and before, the settlement of America. Indeed, the center of Western Civilization was shifting. The Mediterranean has long been the center of civilizations that arose in the West. During the Age of Discovery, or following it, the center of civilization shifted from the Mediterranean to the Atlantic. Up to that time, England had been on the edge of civilization. She was usually at the very end of the trade routes; artistic and intellectual developments reached her shores later than elsewhere, if at all. There was a period during the High Middle Ages when English scholars and thinkers contributed to civilization. Among them were: Anselm of Canterbury, John of Salisbury, Roger Bacon, Robert Grosseteste, Duns Scotus, and William of Ockham. Even then, France, which has ports on the Mediterranean, was much more the leader. In any case, until the 16th century, England was usually on the edge of civilization.

All this was changed following the Age of Discovery and the shift of civilization to the Atlantic. Particularly, the discovery of America placed Britain at one of the focuses of trade routes. More broadly, the English historian, G.M. Trevelyan, has pointed out: "Gradually, during the Tudor reigns, the islanders became aware that their remote situation had changed into a central post of vantage dominating the modern routes of trade and colonization, and that power, wealth and adventure lay for Englishmen at the far end of ocean voyages fabulously long, leading to the gold-bearing rivers of the African...., to the bazaars of jewelled Asia, and to the new half-empty continent which was piecing itself together year by year under the astonished eyes of men...."[4] The time would come, too, when England would itself be the impressive center of civilization, but that was some time in the future.

Sea power really came into its own following upon the Age of Discovery. Before 1500, great military power had been based primarily upon armies. In the following three centuries navies were much more crucial than large armies. The country that dominated the seas might not rule the world, but it certainly had the prime access to world trade and commerce. England was geographically well situated to take advantage of this development.

# Geography of England

England is a part of the continent of Europe, though it is now separated from the continental land mass by the English Channel, which is at its narrowest more than 20 miles across. The country is located on the island of Great Britain. It is probable that Britain was joined to the continent until 8,000 or 10,000 years ago. England occupies the southern and eastern part of Great Britain. To the west lies Wales, and to the north is Scotland. Great Britain is the largest of a chain of islands which, taken together, are known as the British Isles. The other large island is Ireland. From the time of the Roman conquest until the 5th century A.D. what is now England was known as Britain. After the coming of the Angles, Saxons, and Jutes, it became known as England (Angle-Land).

England has by far the most favorable location on Great Britain. Wales and Scotland are hilly and mountainous, and northern Scotland extends into the arctic land-of-the-midnight-sun in summer. Most of the good farming land lies in England, and in the north and west are the hills which contain valuable mineral deposits. The climate of England is usually mild the year around. Though it lies much to the north of New York City, England has warmer winters and cooler summers. The main reason for the mildness of the climate is that it is warmed in winter by the Gulf Stream.

The coastline of England is heavily indented. No place in the country is more than 70 miles from the sea, and there are numerous rivers which provide access to the bodies of water surrounding the island. The rivers and indentions provide many of the good harbors for seaports. It is small wonder, then, that the English became a seafaring people and became deeply involved with trade wherever ships could go.

# English Political System

The English political system grew up, evolved, changed, and developed over many centuries. Although the British speak of the Constitution, they do not have a constitution in the same sense as Americans do. There are great documents which form a part of it, such as the Magna Carta, the Petition of Right, and the Bill of Rights, but the British Constitution is not a written document. Rather, it is a tradition, a collection of practices, a compound of court decisions, a way of doing things politically, to which documents are but footnotes.

Technically, England was a monarchy when the early settlements were made in America. The monarch (king or queen) both reigned and ruled, that is, was head of state and actually governed the people. The powers of the monarch were great at this time. He was head of the Church of England as well as the government. Every act of government was done in his name, and many of those who governed received their appointments from him. He could call Parliament into session, adjourn it, or dismiss it. He could appoint judges and dismiss them, and generally considered that they were supposed to do his bidding.

Monarchy means rule by one. Even at the height of the power of English monarchs, which was around 1600, one-person rule was an exaggeration. Formal acts of the government were usually done by the Crown-in-Parliament. Although the monarch was the dominant figure at this time, constitutionally, England had a *mixed* government. That is, it had elements of monarchy, aristocracy (rule by a few), and democracy (rule by many).

The House of Lords was the aristocratic branch of government. It was made up of the hereditary nobility and the bishops and archbishops of the Church of England. In the early years of James I (reigned 1603-1625), there were 80 nobles in the House. In addition, there were 25 bishops and two archbishops. The monarch was himself chief of the nobles; like them, he was an hereditary aristocrat; and he had the power to increase their number by creating new lords of the realm.

Long before the time of James I, the nobility had lost much of their ancient function. They were no longer warriors, as they had been in the Middle Ages, nor were they great rulers in their own right. But, as Wallace Notestein has pointed out, speaking of one of them: "When Lord Berkeley returning from London came down over the terraces of the Cotswolds to the hundred of Berkeley in the Severn valley, he was met by troops of tenants and retainers. His progress toward his castle was indicated by the peals of bells from the church tower of each village as he reached it. The noble was not the feudal potentate as he had once been, with a body of armed men and a fortified castle, but he was still a magnet of loyalty and a figure of state."[5] Lord Berkeley was a baron, the lowest rank of the nobility. He was a member of the House of Lords, and above him in rank were viscounts, earls, marques, and dukes. Advisers to the monarch usually came from among the Lords at this time.

The House of Commons was the most democratic of the branches. It was made up of men elected from the counties, towns, and universities. In 1603, there were 440 members of the Commons. They were made up of country gentlemen, merchants, and lawyers, among others. Country gentlemen were more numerous; a man did not have to live in the district that elected him, and many of the towns elected people from the country. Commons was becoming more important than it had been earlier in history, but monarchy was still much the most important to the branches of government.

As the above suggests, England still had a very definite class system. The upper classes ruled, and even representatives in the House of Commons were generally people who had considerable land. The class system was maintained by government, and much of it was fixed by law. Heredity was still the main key to what class or rank one belonged to, but other factors might also play a part. For example, Notestein says that technically a country gentleman "was one to whom or to whose ancestors the Heralds' College had granted the right to gentility. That right depended of course upon the possession of a certain amount of property. A country gentleman had lands and tenants and a rent roll of significance."[6] It should be noted, however, that the class system in England at the beginning of the 17th century was not as rigid as it had once been. There were no longer any serfs as such. There were many yeoman farmers, as they were called, who could increase their lands and move up in the scale. Merchants and tradesmen, particularly if they could acquire lands, could become country gentlemen. It had always been possible to rise in the scale as a clergyman, and, though clergy of the Church of England could now marry, positions in the church were not hereditary. Still, the class system was very much supported by law.

## Oppression in England

Not all the English colonies in America were settled because of oppression, but that was the dominant reason for most of them. Thus, it is appropriate to examine some of the ways that the English were oppressed around the time of the early settlements. It should be noted, however, that oppression has not been that uncommon in the course of history. Most people at most times and in most places have been more or less oppressed. Not all of the people are equally oppressed, of course; some are dominant and are highly privileged. This was certainly so in England at the beginning of the 17th century.

It should be noted, too, that people do not always, or even usually, resist oppression. In fact, if they have become used to it over a long period of time they may not even think of it as oppression. It is just the way things are, and most do not spend time imagining them as different. The sense of oppression is usually awakened by changes, and leads to action when there are opportunities for doing something about it. Both of these conditions existed in 17th century England. One thing that was happening was that Puritans and religious dissenters were becoming an increasingly important element. As persecution of these mounted, so did the resistance and the determination to do something

## Sir Edward Coke
## (1552-1634)

An English jurist, most famed for the boost he gave to the common law, Coke was, at various times, member of Parliament, solicitor general, speaker of the House of Commons, attorney general, and Lord Chief Justice of England. His most famous contests were with King James I, and the great issue was whether or not the king was above the law. Coke maintained time and again that James I was bound by the common law. While he did not win in all his contests, he established a sturdy position for future opponents of arbitrary government.

about it. The possibility of settling in America afforded one of the opportunities for doing something about it.

Many Englishmen were inclined to blame the oppressions of the first half of the 17th century on the ruling Stuart monarchs. It is true that James I (1603-1625) insisted upon the full measure of his powers, and that he defended them on the offensive grounds of the Divine Right of Kings. Moreover, Charles I (1625-1649) attempted to rule without going through the motions of using Parliament. But it would be difficult to prove that the Stuarts were more oppressive than the Tudors who preceded them. The Tudors (especially Elizabeth I [1558-1603] had flattered the members of Parliament by having them participate in the often despotic decisions. So far as possible, too, Elizabeth avoided pressing differences to a constitutional crisis. At any rate, there is little reason to doubt that the government of England was often despotic at the outset of the 17th century.

Three different kinds of oppression were particularly troublesome for many of the English. They were political, religious, and economic. All the oppression was by government, of course, and was in a sense political. But what is being called political here is the oppressions carried on against those who were supposed to help with governing. Religious and economic oppression was of a different character.

Although political oppression eventually provoked the greatest resistance in England, it may have been of least importance for colonization. What was involved mainly were the powers, freedom, and independence of the House of Commons and of judges. Members of Commons contended for freedom of speech, that is, the freedom to discuss whatever matters they desired when Parliament was in session, freedom from arrest while Parliament was in session or for what had been said or done there, and the right to initiate and alter legislation that came before them.

Monarchs of the time assumed that they would bring before Parliament such matters as were worthy of consideration and that these might be discussed and decided upon, but no others. Thus, Elizabeth I sent this message to Parliament:

> For liberty of speech her majesty commandeth me to tell you, that to say yea or not to bills. God forbid that any man should be restrained or afraid to answer according to his best liking, with some short declaration of his reason therein, and therein to have a free voice, which is the very true liberty of the house, not as some suppose to speak there of all causes as him listeth [as he wishes], and to frame a form of religion, or a state Government as to their idle brains shall seem meetest. She sayeth no king fit for his state will suffer such absurdities.

James I was even more emphatic, if that is possible, in 1621 when he commanded the Speaker of Commons to "make known in our name unto the House, that none therein shall presume henceforth to meddle with anything concerning our Government or deep matters of State." In other words, all the House need concern itself with was to vote the taxes wanted and go home.

It was under Charles I, however, that the most extensive political persecution occurred. When both houses of Parliament insisted on inquiring into foreign affairs in 1625, Charles dissolved Parliament and had the Speaker of the House of Commons, Sir John Eliot, imprisoned in the Tower of London. Charles badly needed funds, and when Parliament failed to vote them he simply imposed them on his own. Seventy people, including 27 members of Parliament, were sent to prison for refusing to make what they considered unlawful payments to the government. After a stormy session in 1629, Sir John Eliot was once again sent to prison; Parliament was dismissed, and Charles ruled 11 years without it. When Parliament was finally called into session again in 1640, Charles could no longer control its members. Determined resistance was followed by Civil War.

In like manner, the early Stuarts worked to make the courts serve them as they wished. Chief Justice Coke was dismissed by the king for refusing to allow the king to dictate his decisions. Charles I dismissed Chief Justice Crew for refusing to admit the legality of forced loans. He managed to intimidate them so completely during the time that he ruled without Parliament that the courts had become instruments of the despotic will of the king.

The religious oppression of Stuart England is best known to Americans, however, because it was this that drove Pilgrims, Puritans, Baptists, Quakers, and Catholics to migrate in considerable numbers to the New World. Nowhere does the determination to maintain uniformity by stamping out differences appear more clearly.

The Church of England was established by law for all who lived in England. What this meant is well described by Christopher Hill, an English historian. It meant that everyone "had to attend services in his parish church every Sunday, and was liable to legal penalties if he did not. He had to pay tithes, one-tenth of his produce or his profits, to a clergyman whom he had no say in choosing, and of whom he might heartily disapprove. He was liable to the jurisdiction of Church courts, which punished him not only for 'heresy,' nonattendance at church, or sexual immorality, but also for working on Sundays or saints' days, for nonpayment of tithes, sometimes even for lending money at interest." Moreover, the Church kept a close watch over and a tight rein on thought and education. "Books were strictly censored, and the censorship was in the hands of the Bishops. Education was an ecclesiastical [church] monopoly....No person might teach in a school or private family unless licensed by his Bishop."[7]

Anyone who differed from the established church was apt to get into trouble. Dissenters from it, both Protestant and Catholic, were persecuted. During Elizabeth's reign, Catholics were most thoroughly persecuted. An act of 1571 made it treason to declare that Elizabeth ought not to be queen or to bring in a papal decree. An act of 1581 made it a high crime to attempt to convert a subject to the Catholic faith, and set forth penalties for saying or hearing a Mass. During her reign more than 200 Catholics were put to death.

Dissenting Protestants were not spared under Elizabeth either. Some who were not satisfied with the official religion began to hold study meetings. The meetings were called Conventicles. An act of 1593 provided imprisonment for anyone who attended one of these meetings, banishment from England for a second offense, and execution for those who returned to England after having been banished. Matters did not improve much under James I. The Puritans especially hoped that they would, for James had ruled Scotland before becoming king of England. Scotland was Presbyterian, and English Puritans held similar views with them. But James let them know right early that he had had enough of such religion. "No bishop, no king," James told them, and he meant to convey the idea that without a hierarchy ruling the church there was little support for a hierarchy to rule the state.

How little toleration for dissenters there was under James I is suggested by William Bradford, who later came to America. Bradford and a company of dissenters were trying to leave England for Holland in 1608. They arranged with a man for a ship to take them across.

> But when he had them and their goods aboard, he betrayed them, having beforehand...plotted with the searchers and other officers so to do; who took them, and put them into boats, and there rifled and ransacked them, searching to their shirts for money, yea even the women further than became modesty; and then carried them back into the town and made them a spectacle and wonder to the multitude which came flocking on all sides to behold them. Being thus first, by these...officers rifled and stripped of their money, books and much other goods, they were presented to the magistrates....But the issue was that after a month's imprisonment the greatest part [number of them] were dismissed and sent to the places from which they came; but seven of the principal [leaders] were still kept in prison....

Perhaps the most amazing persecution during the reign of James I was that for alleged witchcraft. The belief in witchery had been widespread during the late Middle Ages but had lost much of its appeal as a result of the Renaissance. James revived it in England. He had written a book on demonology before he came to the throne in England. In 1604 he got a law passed increasing penalties against witches, and in the next 12 years many were accused of witchcraft and burnt at the stake.

The persecution of Puritans reached its peak during the 11 years when Charles I ruled without Parliament. Puritans worshiped within the Church of England, but they wanted to change it considerably. They wanted much greater simplicity in services, greater emphasis upon the Bible, and to make the sermon much more central. William Laud, Archbishop of Canterbury, acting under the authority of Charles I, undertook to bring them completely into line or drive them out of England. Visitations were made to churches throughout the country to see that they followed the prescribed rituals, that they did not bring in lecturers on Puritanism, and that they followed the order of service prescribed in the Book of Common Prayer. Those who spread Puritan pamphlets were punished severely by the king's special court. In the decade 1630-1640, thousands of Puritans migrated to New England.

In economic matters, there were considerable resemblances between 17th century England and the 20th century United States. In both, there were major efforts to regulate, control, and direct the economy. Indeed, there are political parallels between 17th century England and 20th century United States. In Europe in general and in England in particular, monarchs claimed near absolute power and to rule by divine right. In 20th century America, the government claims broad and extensive powers but the divine right, if that is the right word, does not belong to monarchs but to the people. But the main subject here is economic oppression in 17th century England.

Two distinct goals underlay the government involvement in the economy. In many respects, they were conflicting goals. One goal was to maintain economic stability, that is, to keep things as they were, to keep people employed at what they had been doing, to keep prices, wages, and production the way they had been. The attempt to do this was largely a relic of Medievalism. On the other hand, the other goal was to spur trade, manufacturing, and foreign commerce. The theory by which this was justified is called mercantilism. Mercantilism was a theory for the government promoting commerce and colonies for the supposed good of the country.

The best known of the attempts to maintain economic stability in England were the laws against enclosure. Enclosure was the practice of combining the many small plots on an estate into a single farm. It was logical for this to be done as serfdom was abolished. However, tenants often had ancient claims to these small plots, and there was resistance to their being enclosed. Hence, laws were passed from time to time restricting enclosure. One of the more determined efforts to prevent enclosure occurred during the reign of Charles I.

There were other attempts to maintain stability as well. Those who governed were "suspicious of social change and social mobility, of the rapid enrichment of capitalists, afraid of the fluctuations of the market and of unemployment...." Thus, "throughout the early Stuart period, governments thought it their duty to regulate industry, wages, and working conditions. In times of dearth [shortage] they ordered Justices of the Peace to buy up corn and sell it below cost price; they forbade employers to lay off workers whose products they could not sell."[8] Fixing wages in those days usually was the reversal of what it is nowadays. The United States government sets minimum wages; the English government usually fixed maximum wages. The price setting on goods in the market was usually similar to what it is in our day, when it occurs.

These government regulations tended to make the market inflexible and led to shortages and surpluses of labor as well as of goods. There was much complaint about it and resistance to it. For example, the Hertfordshire Justices of the Peace complained in 1631 that the regulation of the markets was the reason there was a shortage of goods and prices were so high. The Lancashire Justices of the Peace refused in 1634 to enforce apprenticeship regulations because they said it would cause unemployment. When the government tried to enforce higher wages in Essex, local officials pointed out that less people would be employed at the higher rate.

The mercantilist attempts to advance trade were mostly by way of granting monopolies. A monopoly is an exclusive right to make or sell some good, trade in certain places, or, in the case of colonies, to settle and develop a specific area. Monopolies are ordinarily grants of governments. In early 17th century England it was the habit of monarchs to grant charters or patents to individuals to produce or sell some good (as well as to colonize in some foreign place). According to one compilation, the following items were made monopolies at one time or another during the first 40 years of the 17th century: bricks, glass, coal, iron, tapestries, feathers, brushes, combs, soap starch, lace, linen, leather, gold thread, beaver belts, buttons, pins, dyes, butter, currants, red herrings, salmon, lobsters, salt, pepper, vinegar, tin, beer hops, barrels, bottles, tobacco, dice, cards, pens, writing paper, gunpowder, and so on. Little was left to be monopolized, except bread, as a member of Parliament declared in 1691.

The impact of all these monopolies was such as might have been expected: inconveniences, scarcities, high prices, unemployment, and widespread economic difficulties. The clothing industry was hard hit by the higher prices of soap and alum and by the shortage of potash, which was caused by restrictions on imports. The salt monopoly caused trouble for fishermen. A pamphlet published in 1640 declared that "No freeman of London, after he hath served his years and set up his trade, can be sure long to enjoy the labour of his trade, but either he is forbidden longer to use it, or is forced at length with the rest of his trade to purchase it as a monopoly, at a dear rate, which they and all the kingdom pay for...."

The attempt of the government to give a monopoly to the English in the production of goods could have severe complications. This kind of government intervention even caused a depression during the reign of James I. England had for a long time been a major exporter of cloth. English cloth had usually been sent to the Netherlands for finishing and dyeing. James I became convinced that he and the kingdom would reap great benefits if all this work were done in England. Therefore, he cancelled the privileges of those who had been authorized to export cloth and gave a charter to a new company which could only export finished dyed cloth. The undertaking was a failure. The Dutch prohibited the import of English cloth. In consequence, the foreign market for English cloth dried up; there were 500 bankruptcies and unemployment soared.

There was, then, much oppression and much suffering in England at the time of the early settlement of America.

## *Vitality of the English*

That is, however, but one side of the English story. It is the side which helps to explain why some people left England to settle in America. But to interpret even colonization in terms only of English oppression would be to misunderstand it. The truth is that there was a great vitality in the England of that day. Moreover, there were many signs of increasing pride in being English. Those who came to the New World were proud of their English heritage, determined to preserve the substance of it, for they considered it a goodly heritage. What they considered oppression they were not likely to value, but there was much more than that to being English.

The Englishman of the early 17th century was greatly different from our stereotype of the typical laid-back, cultured, law-abiding Englishman of the 20th century. He was outspoken, argumentative, assertive, adventurous, dogmatic, and often enough tenaciously attached to his beliefs. When the Spanish ambassador threatened Queen Elizabeth with reprisals for holding Spanish ships in port, she told him that if he persisted in talking that way she would have him thrown in a dungeon. Men resisted oppression even as they were being oppressed. They would, and did, go to war for their beliefs, nor were they apt to be shaken from them by the most dreadful punishment. If they were profane, they swore in monstrous oaths; if they were devout, they would put aside all frivolity; if they were seamen, they would sail to any port in the world. If they were farmers, they were looking for more land to cultivate; if they were manufacturers, they were looking to an increase of produce and a broader market. In short, England was a volcano of energy ready to erupt, and erupt it did in a dozen directions in the early 17th century. It was all James I could do to contain the eruptions and Charles I lost his head in trying.

One way to look at the goodly heritage is through the language and literature. English was not a new language, of course. It had emerged in the late Middle Ages, basically German with a strong admixture of French and Latin elements. But it was nearly new as a literary language, still raw, still being shaped, its spelling somewhat uncertain and its structure none too secure. In fact, at the time of the earliest settlements in America master writers were forging it into a powerful literary language. William Shakespeare was still alive when the colony was planted at Jamestown in Virginia.

Even before Shakespeare, though, English was becoming a literary language. Sir Thomas Wyatt (d. 1542) and Henry Howard, the Earl of Surrey (d. 1547) wrote sonnets in English. (Virtually all literature with any pretensions had been written in Latin before this time.) Sir Philip Sidney (d. 1586) wrote a pastoral romance titled *Arcadia*. Edmund Spenser (d. 1599) wrote the *Faerie Queen*, an allegoric poem, which demonstrated what could be achieved in English. But the Elizabethan Age reached its peak in the great dramatists: Thomas Kyd, Christopher

Marlow, Robert Greene and, above all, William Shakespeare (1564-1616).

Shakespeare taught many Englishmen their history from the stage by his plays. From them, they learned of their kings, of John, Henry IV, Henry V, Henry VI, Henry VIII, Richard II, and Richard III, but more important, they learned pride of country, as in these verses from *King John*:

> This England never did, nor never shall,
> Lie at the proud foot of a conqueror...,
> Come the three corners of the world in arms,
> And we shall shock them. Nought shall make us rue,
> If England to itself do rest but true.

Beyond these, Shakespeare left a vast legacy of tragedies and comedies: *Hamlet, Othello, King Lear, Macbeth, The Merchant of Venice,* and *The Tempest.* Man's virtues and vices, nobility and venality, honor and deceit were shriven in unforgettable language in the poetry and prose of Shakespeare.

But one work was vastly more important and had much greater impact on both the English language and men's outlook than all the work of the Elizabethan playwrights, poets and scribblers. In 1611 the King James Version of the Bible was published. It was destined to become *the* Bible of the English speaking people well into the 20th century, and it is still a best seller. There might have been a United States without the King James Version, but it surely would have been somewhat different than it has been. G.M. Trevelyan has well said:

> ...For every Englishman who had read Sidney or Spenser, or had seen Shakespeare acted at the Globe, there were hundreds who had read or heard the Bible with close attention as the word of God. The effect of the continual domestic study of the book upon the national character, imagination and intelligence for nearly three centuries to come, was greater than that of any literary movement in our annals....New Worlds of history and poetry were opened in its pages....Indeed it created the habit of reading and reflection in whole classes of the community....Through the Bible, the deeds and thoughts of men who had lived thousands of years before in the eastern Mediterranean, translated into English during the period when our language reached its brief perfection, coloured the daily thought and speech of Britons, to the same degree as they are coloured in our own day by the commonplaces of the newspaper press....[9]

It is well to know, too, that this literary legacy from England was composed in the last great age of poetry of Western Civilization. At the beginning of the 17th century spoken and written English was alive with poetic expression. By the end of the century, prose had largely replaced it. That is not to say that poetry is not still written, or that poetic expressions do not crop up in our language. But poetry has become a specialized method of writing, remote from the lives of most of us, and prose dominates. Here is an example of poetic thought from the earlier time. It is attributed to Sir Humphrey Gilbert, the man who financed the first expedition aimed at making an English settlement in America. Gilbert wrote to Queen Elizabeth asking her to make haste in granting a charter, for, as he said, "the wings of man's life are plumed with the feathers of death." It is possible to express something of the thought in prose, of course, as "Man's life is lived under the threat of death." But that is hardly to convey the same thing. The sense of mystery and wonder, of the soaring quality of life, of the weight of certain death, of the very vitality that the knowledge that our lifetime is but a brief span gives to life, is missing. The Bible that has been so venerated was translated and the literature of so much influence was composed in a poetic era. That is no small thing.

In no way is the vitality of the English at the time of the settlement of America better exemplified than in the lives and accomplishments of the men of the sea. England was just emerging as a great sea power when the efforts at settlement began. The Spanish dominated the seas for most of the 16th century. Until the middle of that century most English ships rarely ventured voyages of more than a few hundred miles. Mostly, they engaged in journeys along the coastline of northern Europe. During the reign of Elizabeth all that began to change. By the 1580s English ships were turning up at ports around the world. In 1588 a vast Spanish Armada was defeated by the English in the Channel. Naval warfare raged between England and Spain for the next 12 years, and the British emerged triumphant from it. No longer was the path to North America endangered by Spanish ships.

Finally, the following may suggest something of the overall impact of the English heritage upon Americans. Americans think in the ways of Englishmen, some of which might be defined, others not, because they think with the English language. The religious denominations in America were many of them given a particular English turn and coloration. The American colonists tended to accept and preserve English middle class standards, particularly those of the country gentlemen. American political development owes much to England, as may be suggested by the Magna Carta, the Petition of Right, the Bill of Rights, trial by jury, the common law, the writ of habeas corpus, and representative government.

# *Geography of Eastern America*

Eastern North America did not much interest Europeans until more than a century after its discovery. The Cabots had made voyages to this portion of the Americas within a few years of Columbus' initial discoveries much farther to the south. But even the claim that gave to England was largely forgotten until Richard Hakluyt revived the memory of it in the late 16th century. The Cabots were Italian, and no Englishmen had the know-how to repeat the voyage for most of the century that followed. Besides the Spanish would hardly have acknowledged the British claim, and they ruled the seas.

But the British claims aside, the Spaniards were not much interested in the northern reaches of North America. They confined their explorations and such settlements that were made to the deep South and West. That concentration can be accounted for mainly in terms of the geography of Spain and the Americas. A good case can be made that peoples from European countries tended to settle in areas similar to their homeland. Spain is located on a peninsula, the Iberian Peninsula, in southwestern Europe. The climate in Spain is mainly warm and dry. The Spanish settled mostly on peninsula and peninsula-like regions in North America, in Florida and Mexico. By contrast, the British settled first in regions bearing greatest resemblance to their homeland, if we ignore the fact that except for Bermuda they did not settle on islands. England has a heavily indented coastline. So does the region of North America, from the Chesapeake Bay region north to Nova Scotia, which they laid claim to and settled first. Also, these are in a more northerly region than the settlements of Spain, as is Britain. Likewise, the Dutch settled around a great river, the Hudson, which bears a resemblance to their homeland.

There were other reasons, however, for the Spanish focus on southern North America and northern South America. These were the regions generally of the wealthiest and most advanced Indians, the Aztecs in Mexico and the Incas in Peru. They had vast treasures of precious metals, and great wealth poured into Spain for the better part of a century from them. The Indians were generally poor and backward in eastern North America. As the English were to discover, there was not much by way of precious metals to be mined or acquired by conquest there. Except for the great quantities of fish in the ocean off the coast of the northeast there was little of natural resources to attract Europeans.

The Atlantic coast does have many indentions north of the Chesapeake. Many large rivers pour into the bays which empty into the oceans, and these generally make excellent harbors. The rivers had much greater importance than that; they were the highways, so to speak, of that day. Most heavy freight was transported by water until well into the 19th century. Thus most settlements were made either on or near large streams. Undoubtedly, the presense of natural harbors and rivers attracted the English to the places where they settled. For example, there are four large rivers—the Potomac, the Rappahannock, York, and James—which enter the Chesapeake Bay from the south. The first successful English settlement, the one at Jamestown, was made between the York and James rivers.

The topography of eastern North America falls into three regions. Inland from the ocean lies the coastal plain. West of the plain is the Piedmont (foothills) or hill region. West of that are the Appalachian Highlands. The hills and mountains are much nearer to the sea from New York northward. Both the coastal plain and Piedmont are much wider from the Chesapeake Bay southward. The larger rivers are naturally navigable for the width of the coastal plain. The Appalachians formed a natural barrier to settlement west of them during the colonial period, and few people settled on them. In consequence, British settlers congregated along the coast and into the Piedmont. The French, by contrast, came into America by way of the St. Lawrence and spread over a vast area in middle America. The greater density of the British settlements gave them superiority over the French, who were spread out.

The climate in eastern North America is harsher than the English, or western Europeans generally, would have expected. Though England is well to the north of the United States (except for Alaska), the winters are generally much colder and the summers much hotter here than in England. New York City is on about the same latitude as Naples, Italy and Madrid, Spain. Yet heavy snows are common in what became New York state and are rare in England. The harshness of the climate, particularly in the winters, was hard on the early settlers.

East of the Appalachians most of the land was covered by forests, broken only here and there by Indian settlements. As those who tried to lure Europeans to the New World rarely tired of claiming, the oceans were teeming with fish, the woods full of game of all sorts, the land suited to growing many crops, and wild fruits grew in great abundance. Although facts supported these descriptions for the region as a whole, there were areas for which it would be an exaggeration. Moreover, that wood was so plentiful might have seemed a boon to Englishmen for whom it was scarce, but in fact forests were mainly an obstacle to the early settlers. They had to be cleared before the land could be cultivated.

Historians and others have often claimed in the 20th century that the great wealth of the people in the United States could be attributed mainly to the abundance of natural resources in America. That is a highly questionable claim. It ignores the struggle, the ingenuity, and the tenacity involved in producing wealth in America. It confuses the puffery of those attempting to lure settlers to America with the hardship, suffering, and perseverance that was often involved in even getting a living. Viewing America, such of it as was known in 1600, few could or did predict any vast wealth in that region that is now the United States. The native inhabitants provided few clues to it. They were almost uniformly poor and backward. Undoubtedly, there were many *potential* resources in America, as there are in most regions of the world. But the significance of that only becomes clear by exploring the meaning of what we call natural resources.

The phrase natural resources can easily convey the wrong impression. It would be much more precise to call them natural *materials*. Natural materials only become resources when uses are found for them and, usually, when they are developed. For example, is a tree a resource or an obstacle? That depends. It depends upon whether we wish to cut wood for a fire or plant crops where it stands. Is a river a resource or an obstacle? That depends upon whether you are traveling by boat or by a wheeled vehicle. Is oil a resource or a nuisance? That depends upon whether you are digging for water or have developed ways of refining it and burning it for heat, light, or locomotion. Undoubtedly, all these are materials found in nature, but they are only resources, actually, when uses have been found or developed for them.

It is misleading, then, to ascribe American wealth to natural resources. Wealth comes from the utilization of materials found in nature, from the resourcefulness in finding uses for them, not from natural resources. This is a point that will come up in other ways in recounting American history.

## *The American Indian*

Nowadays the Indians are often referred to as "native Americans." That way of putting it is accurate enough when comparing the Indians to those who came to the New World in the 16th century and afterward. However, though there is no doubt that they were the earlier inhabitants, even discoverers, of America, it is generally believed that they, too, were once immigrants to America. That is, they migrated to this land though it must have been thousands of years ago.

It should be emphasized, however, that we have no certain knowledge of the origins of the Indians. The belief that they migrated from elsewhere to the Americas is based on speculation. This speculation is hinged on the belief in the common origin of mankind. Such evidence as there is to support the view that the Indians came from elsewhere is mainly negative. There is no historical record at all, either in the Old

World or the New, of any such migration. The negative evidence, which is not, properly speaking, evidence at all, for the migration(s) is that no relics of early man have been discovered in America. There is, then, no positive proof one way or the other for the speculation.

However, if the belief that the Indians migrated to the Americas be accepted or assumed, a quite plausible explanation of how it occurred can be and has been constructed. The most widely accepted speculation is that they crossed to North America from Asia on the tail end of the last Ice Age. They could have crossed mainly on ice along the line of the Aleutian Islands, say, to the mainland in Alaska. They could have come in a succession of migrations, separated by hundreds of years, and fanned out over the continents. The most that can be said for this speculation is that if the migration(s) did occur it might have happened that way.

What is not in doubt is that there were human inhabitants in the Americas and the surrounding islands when the Europeans came. Beyond that, there is legendary and archeological evidence of some developments going back a few hundred years. The highest developments had or were occurring in Central America and what is now Mexico and Peru. The ones that concern us most here, however, are those that lived in eastern North America.

The Indians of eastern America were at a level of development that might be best described as neolithic. The late anthropologist Ralph Linton says that when the "Spanish explorers reached these shores, the peoples of America had arrived at the stage of civilization which Southwest Asia had attained in 3500 B.C. and Western Europe in 1500 B.C."[10] That is to say that they were hardly civilized at all, and, since he was generalizing for all the Indians, the dates should probably be pushed back a bit. At any rate, they were hunters and fishers, which they supplemented with rudimentary farming. Their organization was tribal, and they lived in villages under the authority of a chieftain. War was commonplace; indeed, it might be described as normal. Historian Samuel Eliot Morison says, "Not all Indians lived in a continual state of intertribal war, but war was part of the social pattern. Bringing back scalps was equivalent to a high school certificate for the young braves ....Any Indian group that tried to shift its dominant values from war to peace was doomed to extinction by another."[11]

Except for those within their own tribes, Indians had little or no sense of kinship with one another or that they belonged to the same race. When they first encountered Europeans, they were more likely to be friendly than not, and inclined to view them as potential allies against their regular Indian enemies. However, their friendliness was usually shortlived, and many Indian tribes very readily made war on white men, even as they did other Indians.

Although Indians rarely were organized beyond the local tribe, they have been classified by language groupings. On this basis there were three major groups in eastern America at the time that the Europeans came: the Algonquian, Iroquois, and Muskhogean. The Algonquian tribes could be found all the way from Nova Scotia to Virginia and into the Midwest. Perhaps the best known of these tribes were the Delaware and Powhatan. The Powhatan were the Indians encountered by the settlers at Jamestown. They lived in wigwams or, more descriptively, longhouses. These were constructed with poles bent from either side to make a semicircular roof, and the poles were covered with bark. These houses were often extended to considerable length and inhabited by several families, hence longhouses. They farmed, hunted, and fished for their livelihood. Their clothes, such as they were, were made from animal skins and furs. The men wore only the briefest of clothing, even in winter.

The Iroquois Indians were located mainly in New York and Pennsylvania. There was an Iroquois confederation made up of five tribes, or nations, as they were sometimes called: the Mohawk, Cayuga, Oneida, Onondaga, and Senaca. The Cherokee Indians in the South were also of Iroquois stock. The Muskhogean Indians, which included the Choctaws, Creeks, Chickasaws, and Seminoles, were located in what is now the southeastern United States. They were the most admired by the European settlers of the Indians in the east, not only for their skills as potters, weavers, and farmers, but also because they learned readily from the settlers and adopted many of their ways. They were referred to as the civilized tribes. However, settlers made contact with these Indians much later than the others, and had generally formed their opinions of Indians before making the acquaintance of these.

The only means of transport the Indians had was the canoe. None of the Indians anywhere had the wheel or wheeled vehicles. There were no large draft animals in all the Americas, and the largest domesticated animal in North America was the dog. They had nowhere developed an alphabet, and the only writing that has been discovered was possibly at the level of Egyptian hieroglyphics among the Indians of Central America. These, too, have developed a calendar. The Indians of eastern America had stone and wood implements and pottery.

There was a great cultural as well as technological gap between the European settlers and the American Indians. It was much wider for the English in eastern North America than it was for the Spanish in Mexico and Peru, because the Indians were not so far advanced. It may be possible to imagine that the English settlers and Indians could have lived peacefully side by side in America. But to do so is to ignore the cultural gap which separated them from one another. Some examples will illustrate the problem. The early settlers had instructions to purchase the land they settled from the Indians. That, however, was easier said than done. On many occasions, white men made what they understood to be purchases and Indians accepted their offers of payment. But neither could grasp the nature of the transaction the other thought he was making. The Algonquians, for instance, had a strong belief that the land was theirs, though they did not consider it individually owned private property. But they had no such concept as selling the land and alienating it from themselves. At most, they could only have been leasing rights on something like a temporary basis. After all, Indians did not have land surveyors, make deeds, or have a complex system of laws.

The problem was more basic than that, however. The colonists and the Indians had different and conflicting concepts for using the land. So far as the English settlements were financed in England, and most of them were at the outset, they were commercial ventures. As soon as the colonists began to rely on farming, they were doing so to raise a surplus for sale elsewhere. To succeed, they put more and more land under cultivation. By contrast, Indians only farmed small plots and relied on hunting for their clothes and much of their food. These different usages on adjacent lands do not go well together. Large numbers of wild animals are a threat to crops. On the other hand, private owners of land would resent Indians coming on their land to hunt, even where forests were left standing. In short, commercial farming and subsistence hunting do not go together.

Other examples could be given illustrating the cultural gap, but perhaps the conclusion can be drawn from what has been said. For the settlers and the Indians to live peacefully side by side one or the other would have to change their ways. Even with the best of will that would have been difficult for either to do over a long period of time and virtually impossible over the short run. Even if the English colonists had been free to abandon commercial farming, for example, which they were not, it is doubtful if they would have adopted Indian ways. They were convinced of their superiority to the Indians generally and were determined to preserve their heritage. Most Indians clung no less tenaciously to their habits, their customs, their ancient ways, and so forth. In consequence, there were battles, wars, mutual hatreds, and other conflicts until the Indians were conquered and moved away.

That is not to say that the colonists did not learn from the Indians or, conversely, that the Indians did not learn much from the settlers. They both did. The most direct influence of the Indians on the colonists was agricultural products and methods. Among the crops developed by the Indians and adopted by the settlers somewhere in the Americas were: corn, several varieties of beans, pumpkins, chocolate, quinine, rubber, squash, potatoes, tomatoes, and tobacco. Corn was grown by

Indians throughout the Americas in temperate and tropical climates. The Indians called it maize, and writers sometimes refer to it as Indian corn. The latter phrase may be confusing to Americans, who might suppose that there are, or were, other varieties of what they call corn. That is not the case. Corn was native to the Americas and was not grown anywhere else in the world until after the discovery of America. The difficulty is with the term "corn," not with the facts. The English used the term to refer to grains in general or to the dominant grains grown in an area, as wheat and barley, for example. In English translations of the Bible, for example, there are references to corn, and even ears of corn, in the ancient Mediterranean region. The reference is to grains of some sort, not to what Americans call corn.

Although "Indian corn" is now grown in many parts of the world, it is hardly to exaggerate to say as one writer does that "Maize was, in a sense, the bridge over which European civilization travelled to a foothold in the new world. To many of the early colonists, who learned its culture from the Indians, it became the daily bread by which they were nourished. Modern American agriculture is founded to a large extent upon an elaborate cultural complex taken from the American Indians, for not only did the European colonist adopt the maize plant; he also embraced the methods of culture, harvesting and utilization which the Indian had developed through generations of trial and error."[12]

Aside from corn, the other crop grown by the eastern North American Indians which became of such great commercial importance was tobacco. Tobacco—the "noxious weed," as James I called it—was introduced in England by Sir Walter Raleigh. The demand for it rose

## Sir Walter Raleigh (circa 1552-1618)

Raleigh was a man of vast energy and numerous undertakings: sailor, soldier, pirate, soldier of fortune, explorer, politician, colonizer, courtier, and writer. He caught Queen Elizabeth's attention with his good looks and dashing ways, and she lavished estates and offices on him. It was the queen's favor which enabled him to attempt to plant a colony in North Carolina. However, he lost her good will, never had that of James I, and spent a good many years imprisoned in the Tower of London. It was there that he wrote his *History of the World*, which was long a popular book. Eventually, James I had him executed for encroaching upon Spanish claims in South America.

swiftly. Eastern Indians also grew pumpkins and beans, among other vegetables, but most of the other products came from elsewhere in the Americas. The tomato grew in tropical climates, was early taken to Europe, but did not begin to become an important crop in the United States until the late 19th century. The (white) potato apparently originated in South America. It was probably introduced into Europe in the middle of the 16th century, but it may not have been brought into the English colonies before 1719. Seeds were brought from Ireland on that date, and it was widely called the "Irish" potato, a distinction which still survives in the South. The other products come from Latin America.

Such agricultural methods as killing trees by girdling, fertilizing with fish, planting beans and pumpkins in corn, preserving corn in ventilated cribs, and storing potatoes in pits were learned from the Indians.

Indian influence is also apparent in many place names which are Indian words, or corruptions of them. Streams and rivers frequently bear Indian names, and from these, quite often, come the Indian names of towns and cities, counties, and states. For example, in the county in which the present writer lives, there is a creek by the name of Wehadkee, a river named Tallapoosa, and the county seat is Wedowee, all Indian names. Many well-known cities, such as Chicago, and rivers, such as the Mississippi and Ohio, bear Indian names. Indian names are less common for places on the east and west coast of the United States. In the original 13 colonies English place names are much more common; on the west coast, Spanish names predominate in California.

Deeper influences of the Indians are both more difficult to detect and to prove. Some suppose that Indian confederations, such as that of the Iroquois, may have influenced the confederation of the states under the Articles of Confederation or even our federal system of government. Evidence for this is hard to come by. Confederations have been familiar in Europe since the time of the ancient Greeks. European confederations were the ones discussed at length in the Constitutional Convention. Pending better proofs of deeper Indian influences than we now have, the main conclusion to be drawn is that the predominant influences on European settlers were, and remained, European, that they resisted Indian culture, usually refused to "go native," and were probably more influenced by the conflicts with them than by imitation.

Many Indians have also clung to and tried to preserve their native cultures for a period of several centuries. On the whole, though, they have been much more deeply influenced by the white man than otherwise. Large numbers of Indians eventually accepted the dominant culture as their own. Many have become Christians. Most speak the English language, but if they have any other written language it is in the European alphabet. In truth, there was much more to be learned from European civilization than Indian culture.

# Chapter 4
# The Establishment of the Colonies

*Being thus arrived in good harbor, and brought safe to land, they fell upon their knees and blessed the God of Heaven who had brought them over the vast and furious ocean, and delivered them from all the perils and miseries thereof, again to set their feet on the firm and stable earth, their proper element....*

*What could now sustain them but the Spirit of God and His grace? May not and ought not the children of these fathers rightly say: "Our fathers were Englishmen which came over this great ocean, and were ready to perish in this wilderness; but they cried unto the Lord, and He heard their voice and looked on their adversity.... Yea, let them which have been redeemed of the Lord, shew how He hath delivered them from the hand of the oppressor...."*

**—William Bradford, 1620**

---

## Chronology

1607—Settlement of Jamestown.

1619—Calling of legislative assembly in Virginia.

1620—Landing of Pilgrims at Plymouth.

1624—Virginia becomes a Royal Colony.

1630—Beginning of Massachusetts Bay Colony.

1634—Settlement in Maryland.

1635—Settlement of Connecticut.

1636—Founding of Rhode Island.

1649—Maryland Act of Toleration.

1664—English Conquest of New Netherland.

1663—Settlement of the Carolinas.

1676—Bacon's Rebellion.

1681—Founding of Pennsylvania.

1732—Settlement of Georgia.

Attempts to make settlements in the New World were perilous and precarious undertakings in the early 17th century. The English had made several attempts at colonizing before 1607, but all of them had failed for one reason or another. That further attempts would meet with any other fate was hardly a foregone conclusion. We know now, of course, that the settlement made at Jamestown in 1607 would be permanent, but that only became certain after the development, that is, after it became history. For several years after the first settlers arrived the success of the undertaking was very much in doubt.

One of the great difficulties was crossing the ocean. Although voyages between the Old and New World had become common enough (for sailors anyway), they were still fraught with peril. The ships were small, made of wood, and powered by wind caught in sails. Ocean-going vessels today are commonly a *thousand* times the size of those around the turn of the 17th century. A small ship might displace 10 tons, then, and one today will usually displace 10,000 tons. A large ship, then, might displace 100 tons; nowadays, there are tankers more than 1,000 times that in size. Such vessels were not only quite limited in the number of people they could carry but also in the amount of the cargo. Voyages of two months or more were not unusual; so much depended upon the wind and the weather. Sailings were infrequent in the early years of settlement, so that people might wait for a year or longer for new provisions or reinforcements from England.

Once they had arrived in the New World, settlers had large problems of surviving. Such provisions as they brought with them often spoiled during the crossing. Even if they arrived during the early part of the growing season, land would still have to be cleared for crops. Shelters had to be built, food had to be somehow acquired, and provision made for the winter. Widespread and deadly illnesses were common during the first year, attributable to exposure in unfamiliar climates, exertion, and diseases for which they had built up no immunities.

There were dangers, as well, from other European settlers and from potentially hostile Indians. When the war between England and Spain ended in 1604, the Spanish did not make concessions about English claims in the New World. Thus, English colonists might be challenged by the Spanish. In addition, the French, and especially the Dutch, were interested in trading and colonizing in North America. Sometimes trade with Indians enabled settlers to survive; at others, Indian raids threatened the colonists and decimated populations. The building of stockades and maintaining security against Indians occupied valuable time needed for peaceful pursuits.

It is appropriate, then, to ask these questions. In view of all the dangers and uncertainties, what moved the people to attempt settlements in America? Why would they leave their homes to cross the vast ocean and encounter predictable and unpredictable hardships? What spirit, hope, expectation, and quest brought shipload after shipload of settlers to this country?

The first thing to note is that the English settlements in America were from first to last basically commercial undertakings. That does not mean that the economic motive was the primary or only one for the settlers themselves. It does mean that those who financed the settlements hoped for profit and gain. Usually, they were financed by men of considerable wealth, and more often than not they remained in England. All the settlements were privately financed. The government in England neither paid for the undertakings, guaranteed their success, nor offered material aid to those who financed or settled the colonies. The king issued charters which included grants of lands to the companies who would make settlements, but the claims to the land granted had no foundation in actual control, and kings sent neither armies nor navies to bring the territory under their control.

Probably the greatest hope for gain at the outset was that the settlers would discover gold or other precious metals. They had before them the model of Spain, whose *conquistadores* had found great riches in gold in the New World. They might also trade with the Indians, especially for furs or any products wanted in the Old World. Beyond that, there was hope for the development of forest products which were in short supply in England. Individual settlers were often drawn with promises of land. Land had long been the way to prestige and power as well as wealth, and even modest landholdings were much sought after in England. What opportunities there might be for improving one's financial position was an open question, at the least. It should be noted, too, that whatever may have moved particular people to come to America, everyone had to have the means to live, and it was hardly possible to provision them from England in the 17th century. In short, whether they came to America to improve themselves economically or not, they had to find means to provide for themselves and their families.

Religion played a large role in the settlement of America, more in some colonies than others, but it was an important factor in all colonies. Interest in and concern about religion was especially strong in the 17th century. The Puritans were gaining in numbers and influence in the first half of the century; religious wars raged in Europe in the 1630s and 1640s; and several splinter denominations were gaining followers in England. Religious oppression, described earlier, led many to seek refuge in America. Many came for freedom to practice their particular religious beliefs. It would not be correct, however, to describe this as coming for religious freedom in general. At the beginning of the century, hardly anyone thought it would be possible to have a community in which people held different, or no, religious beliefs. There was little enough desire for religious toleration at the time, much less religious liberty. What those settlers came for, then, who sought religious refuge in America, was to form communities in which they would worship and live according to their beliefs.

But whether they were dissenters from the Church of England or not, religion played a prominent role in the lives of settlers. Attendance upon religious services was required of the settlers at Jamestown, though they were not dissenters. The charters authorizing settlement usually contained statements to the effect that one of their purposes was to carry the Gospel to the heathen Indians. While there is no good reason to doubt that this was an imperative motive for the more devout, they were too preoccupied with more pressing matters during the early years to do much about it. Many were sustained during the hardships of the early years by their faith, too.

The lure of adventure undoubtedly drew some men to join these daring enterprises. The very difficulties were a challenge, and overcoming them, if not a sufficient reward in itself, a reward nonetheless. To explore, to learn about, and perchance to report to their countrymen strange and unknown territories and peoples was a motive for some. In any case, security was not an ideal in that day, as it has become in ours; masculine virtues prevailed; the uncertainty of life was a given, accepted and acted upon, not avoided.

## *Virginia*

English America *was* Virginia in 1606, and for several years thereafter. It was called by that name. It had been named for Queen Elizabeth, the virgin queen. The first English child born in America, born to Ananias and Ellinor Dare on Roanoke Island in 1587, was named Virginia. When charters were granted for settlements in America to the London and Plymouth companies in 1606, portions of Virginia were divided between them. That portion assigned to the Plymouth (New England) company was referred to for some time as Northern Virginia. The Plymouth company attempted a settlement in what is now the state of Maine, but it was abandoned after a year or so. The London company, which had been granted lands around the Chesapeake Bay, financed the settlement at Jamestown, which became the first permanent colony in English America. It was located in what is now the state of Virginia.

These facts may serve to emphasize the premier role of Virginia in American history for the first 200 years or more. It is not difficult to establish the fact that Virginia (the colony and later state, not the imaginary Virginia of 1606) was the leader in many respects throughout the colonial period and in the early years of the Republic. The first permanent settlement was made in Virginia, the first major staple crop for trade grown there, the first legislative assembly held there, the first Crown colony established there, the model for colonial governments placed in operation there, and it became eventually the most populous colony. In the founding of the United States, Virginians played a leading role: a Virginian wrote the Declaration of Independence, was commander of the Continental Army, was most often called "the father of the Constitution," was first President of the United States, and four of the first five Presidents were Virginians.

In one crucial major respect, however, Virginia was not the leader. It did not lead in the founding of educational institutions, in the publishing of books, or in the writing of American history. Massachusetts took an early lead there, and held it for much of the history of this country. For this reason, students have often encountered a distortion in their history books. The Pilgrims and Puritans play a larger role in our conception of colonial history than is warranted by the facts. For example, most people know the name of the ship—the *Mayflower*—on which the Pilgrims came to America; few know the names of the ships—*Susan Comfort, Goodspeed* and *Discovery*—on which the first settlers came to Virginia. At the least, this work will attempt to balance the accounts.

The London company got together an expedition for America in late 1606, but it did not sail until early the next year. It reached the Chesapeake Bay in April of 1607 and chose a location on the James (named for the reigning King James I) River. The settlers were beset with difficulties from the outset. The several men placed in charge quarreled among themselves. Their location may have been well chosen for reaching it by ship, but the area was swampy, low lying and hard to defend. The ships left 104 men behind in June, and the group had been reduced to 46 by September. What it was like for the next several months is well told in the words of one who was there:

> There were never Englishmen left in a foreign country in such misery as we were in this new discovered Virginia. We watched every three nights lying on the bare cold ground, what weather soever came...; which brought our men to be most feeble wretches. Our food was but a small can of barley, sodden in water to five men a day. Our drink, cold water taken out of the river; which was at flood very salt: at low tide full of slime and filth, which was the destruction of many of our men. Thus we lived for the space of five months in this miserable distress, not having five able men to man our bulwarks upon any occasion.

Cold statistics give some idea of the hardship, suffering and death in the early years of Virginia. In 1623, a royal commission investigated the conduct of the colony to that point. It noted that from 1607 to 1623 approximately 5,500 persons had located in the colony. Three hundred of these had returned to England at one time or another, and there were about 1,200 living there in 1623. Thus, about 4,000 people had died in a span of 17 years. Some of these died in particularly dramatic circumstances. There was the "starving time" in the winter 1609-1610. This was preceded by harsh treatment by the Indians: a trading expedition to the Indians was slain; the Indians killed and carried off their domestic animals and even drove the deer away from the camp. The settlers were in such straits that they killed and ate the horses and dogs and even resorted to eating mice and snakes. Another dramatic episode took place in 1622 when Indians attacked by surprise and massacred at least 347 persons.

## Sir Thomas Dale
## (died 1619)

Dale was a British naval commander who governed the Virginia colony 1611-1616. He did manage to bring some order to the colony, but he did so only by tyrannical rule. A set of laws, entitled "Articles, Laws, and Orders—Divine, Political, and Martial," was decreed. Their severity was less burdensome, however, because Dale began to allow private landholding. After he left Virginia, he was placed in command of a British fleet, an undertaking more in keeping with his temperament.

Some of the suffering and hardship in the colony may have been unavoidable. For example, the Indians resented not only the encroachment of the settlers in their country but also the indications that they were permanent. But much of the trouble was caused by misdirected and tyrannical control over the colony. Although the settlers were granted by charter "all Liberties, Franchises, and Immunities," the king assured them, "as if they had been abiding and born within this our Realm of England," the words were hardly respected in the first years. The settlers were treated as if they were servants of the company living under martial law. They had no private property in land or crops, were given no opportunity to provide for themselves, and received provisions from a common storehouse. The laws were harsh, and the settlers had no way to alter them. Under Sir Thomas Dale, such laws as these held sway: "Swearing was punished by death, and all the colonists were required to attend religious service regularly; for the first offense a man lost his rations, for a second offense he was whipped, and for a third offense he was sent to the gallows. Unlicensed trade with the Indians was punished by death. Avoidance of labor was punished by imprisonment and, if repeated, by death. Rebels were to be broken on the wheel..., and they were then to be chained to a tree until they died.''[13]

On top of all this, the settlers were kept too busy with unfruitful undertakings to be productive in the first years, even if there had been proper incentives. Expeditions were sent out in futile efforts to find gold. They searched too, or were supposed to, for the mythical North- west Passage. (The hope persisted for many years that a water route to the Pacific would be found through the continent. This was a relic of Columbus' dream of finding a practical route to the East by sailing west from Europe.) The most energetic of the early leaders was Captain John Smith. He was placed in charge of the colony in 1608, and proceeded to direct affairs to achieve some success. However, he had to leave for England in 1609, and the situation deteriorated swiftly after he left.

Two major developments occurred between 1612-1618 to improve conditions in Virginia. One was the cultivation and sale of tobacco. John Rolfe, who married the Indian princess Pocahontas, began to cultivate tobacco. Others would have followed suit, and quickly, but Governor Dale clamped down on the activity. When he was replaced in 1616 by a more lenient leader, planters turned to raising tobacco as a mainstay. The other development was well under way by this time. It was the abandonment of the practice of placing all goods in a common storehouse and the shifting to private ownership and enterprise. The common storehouse approach has sometimes been called communism, but in the circumstances it could more accurately be styled *corporatism*. The idea with which the colony was started was that everything pro- duced belonged to the company. As compensation for this, the com- pany was supposed to provide for the settlers.

But whatever it should be called, there is general agreement that it did not work well. An observer on the scene in 1614 said that "When our people were fed out of the common store and labored jointly in the manuring of ground and planting corn,... the most honest of them..., would not take so much faithful and true pains in a week as...he will do in a day" on his own crop.[14] A modern historian has summed up the situation this way: "This plan did not yield good results. In Virginia the settlers 'loafed on the job,' since they got a living, irrespective of their personal efforts. They could receive but little, if any, benefit from the colony's surplus; hence a surplus was not produced."[15] That understates the case, however. It was not simply a matter of producing a surplus; quite often, they did not have the means on hand to survive the winter. It was more the case that until individuals could manage their own affairs they could neither provide well for themselves or others.

## John Smith
## (circa 1579-1631)

Smith rose from obscure beginnings in England to become a soldier, soldier of fortune, explorer, colonizer, and, above all, a publicist, both of himself and of English settlement in America. At Jamestown, he was among the original settlers and a member of the governing body, and head of it, 1608-1609. A few years later, he made an exploring voyage to the as yet unsettled New England region. Smith's published works include: *General History of Virginia, A Map of Virginia,* and *A Description of New England.* He fixed the name New England on that region.

Although Governor Dale was best known for oppressive acts he did begin to modify the common system so as to permit the settlers to have small tracts of land from which they could have most of the produce. By the 1620s all the land had come into private ownership. By that time the colony had begun to prosper, especially through the tobacco trade, though the company never turned a profit. In 1624, Virginia was taken out of the control of the company and became a Crown colony.

Meanwhile, another important development had taken place. In 1619 a call was sent out by the company for a legislative assembly to be elected. Representatives to it were elected by virtually all the men in the colony. It was the first such assembly in English America and was the forerunner of popularly elected legislatures in this country. From time to time assemblies met over the next couple of decades until the government was regularized in 1639. The governor was instructed in that year to summon representatives from "all and singular plantations there, which together with the governor and council shall have power to make acts and laws for the government of that plantation, correspondent as near as may be to the laws of England." (This assembly was called the House of Burgesses. It should be noted, too, that colonies were often referred to as "plantations" in the early 17th century. Later the term was used to refer to large farms in the South.)

By the 1630s Virginia was well established as a permanent colony. In the course of its establishment the basic pattern for the relation of a colony to the mother country had been worked out. That a colony should make its own laws for governing within the colony, that these should be in accord with English law, and that the colony should benefit the mother country economically, was now on record. Though not all colonies would conform to this prescription, it was the basic pattern.

# New England

To say that Virginia was settled first in time and, at the crucial times, the leading state in the formation of the United States, is not to minimize the importance of Massachusetts and of New England generally. In fact, if New England had been as closely attached to old England and the British Empire as were some of the colonies to the South, there might never have been a United States. At any rate, the virtual independence of New England colonies from England for a portion of their history counted for much eventually. Moreover, the New England colonies were more closely tied to one another than were the colonies elsewhere. They have more nearly a common history, and it is fitting to discuss them in relation to one another.

Massachusetts was the first colony settled, and the others were mostly offshoots from it. For most of the colonial period the New England colonies were Massachusetts, Rhode Island, New Hampshire, Connecticut and, at statehood time, Maine and Vermont. The most distinctive feature of New England was the religious impetus behind so many of the settlements there. While religion was important in all colonies, and in some of the communities founded in others, it was a major factor in settlers coming to New England; in no others was the sense of religious mission so strong. It is not going too far to say that the fairest flower of English Protestantism flowered in New England.

Although Europeans had been attracted to the fisheries off the New England coast even in the 16th century, making permanent settlements was another matter. The winters were harsh by western European standards, certainly by those of the English, and the land was not likely to yield much that was in demand in Europe, even if a surplus could be produced. The early settlements that had been undertaken had failed, and even the Pilgrims who made what was to become a permanent settlement in 1620 at Plymouth may have intended to settle much farther to the south. If they did, they kept it a secret until they landed.

One thing is certain, their charter called for them to settle in Virginia, not near Jamestown, but far to the south of where they settled. Thus, it was necessary for them to get a new charter in 1621 for the area in which they settled. They were called Pilgrims (wanderers, so to speak) because some of them had earlier migrated to Holland to find a place where they could worship according to their beliefs, had returned to England because of their desire to preserve their Englishness, and then migrated to America. They were called Separatists in religion, because they had separated from the established Church of England. They believed in the independence of each congregation.

Their minister was William Brewster, and, after the death of their first governor in 1621, William Bradford became the leader of this settlement for the rest of his life. There was much suffering in the first winter at Plymouth, and half of those who came died. However, the next year conditions improved: the Indians came to their aid, and a new shipload of settlers from England arrived. At first, Plymouth had a common system of working and sharing of the produce, similar to the practice at first in Jamestown. Their charter did provide that after seven years of service, those who persevered might have land of their own. However, the settlers were discontented with the common system almost from the beginning. Able bodied men complained that they did the work but received no more than those who did little or none. The older and more experienced were reduced to the same level as the young. Moreover, wives were expected to wash the clothes, dress the meat, and serve in such ways all the inhabitants. This was more than the women or their husbands could gladly tolerate. In consequence, Governor Bradford began to allow families to have their own crops in 1623 and to parcel out some of the land in 1624. Much fuller division was accomplished when the Pilgrims in America bought out the London financiers of the project.

## William Bradford
## (1590-1657)

Bradford was with the Pilgrims on their sojourn in the Netherlands and came with them on the *Mayflower* to Plymouth. He was elected governor of the Plymouth colony in 1621, and served in that position most years until his death. In both religious and political matters, Bradford led the colony during the founding decades. He took the leadership in putting it on a sound economic footing by establishing private land owning, and cooperated but did not unite with the Massachusetts Bay colony.

But the Pilgrims were few in number compared to the Puritans who flooded into Massachusetts in the years 1630-1642. Two hundred ships brought 20,000 settlers during this 12-year period. New England would surely have remained a backwater settlement area for many years had it not been for this large migration. The migration paralleled closely the period in England under Charles I when the king ruled without Parliament. The Puritans had been gaining in influence just before this time, but now they were being excluded from any participation in rule. But even as Charles I foreclosed their opportunities at home he opened up a fertile field for the Puritans abroad. It was surely no accident that when

Charles I dissolved Parliament in early March 1629, it was followed within a few days by the granting of a royal charter to the Puritan controlled Massachusetts Bay Company. Clearly, he followed a course designed to rid himself of the boldest and most troublesome of the Puritans.

Even so, there was one strange feature of the charter. Contrary to established practice, it did not require that the company hold its meetings in England. In the first few months, nothing was made of this situation. The company remained in England and planted a settlement at Salem in Massachusetts. But by October an important change had been made through the efforts of John Winthrop and some of the more determined Puritans in the company. The members of the company had agreed that both the charter and the company would be located in Massachusetts. John Winthrop was elected governor. When the move had been accomplished, Massachusetts was not so much a colony as an independent country or commonwealth. Even before these events, the colony at Plymouth had attained its independence from the company which had settled it. But whatever the legal status of Massachusetts, those in charge framed their own laws and governed themselves and the inhabitants without consulting king or Parliament for a good many years.

The Puritans had been mostly in the established church in England. However, they had been much influenced by Calvinism and sought to "purify" the church, that is, restore it to the simplicity and the biblical foundations of early Christianity. They had been thwarted in their efforts at change in the 1620s, and those who came to America were ready to separate entirely from the Church of England and follow their own congregational pattern.

The leaders of the settlement in Massachusetts had a strong sense of religious mission. They were rooted in the idea of a long history of persecution and suffering, going back to Moses and the children of Israel and forward through the persecution of the early Christians and down to their own experience. As one historian says, "New Englanders read sympathetically the Old Testament epic of the Israelites wandering through the wilderness to a promised land under the guidance of God.... Since the Hebrews had forfeited their central role in history, the Puritans were now the Chosen People, the Choice Seed, the Elect, for they were guided...by a new Moses, William Bradford to Plymouth, and by another, John Winthrop to the Massachusetts Bay Colony."[16] Their sense of mission was sharpened, too, by trends in England and on the continent of Europe in the 1620s and 1630s. The Protestants were threatened with destruction by Catholic armies in the Thirty Years' War on the continent. England was cracking down on non-conformists at home. The time was at hand, the leaders thought, to set up a place for the propagation of what they conceived to be the true religion far from the persecutions of the old world.

The Puritans intended to establish a theocracy, i.e., rule by God through the elect, those chosen by Him, and in the early years they went a long way toward doing so. Their mission was to live according to God's ways. John Winthrop put it this way:

> Thus stands the cause between God and us. We are entered into a covenant with Him for this work. We have taken out a commission. The Lord hath given us leave to draw our own articles.... We have hereupon besought Him of favor and blessing. Now if the Lord shall please to hear us, and bring us in peace to the place we desire, then hath He ratified this covenant and sealed our commission, and will effect a strict performance of the articles contained in it: but if we shall neglect the observation of these articles..., the Lord will surely break out in wrath against us; be revenged of such a sinful people, and make us know the price of the breach of such a covenant.[17]

Understanding the doctrine of the covenant is necessary both to a grasp of the Puritan mission and to the meaning of a constitution in America. The doctrine of the covenant is that people may make an agreement with God and with one another. It is similar to a contract among men, but much more profound. For by a covenant men bind themselves to God to do his will, and God binds Himself to them. There are overtones of this doctrine in such great documents as the Mayflower

## John Winthrop
## (1588-1649)

Winthrop was trained for and practiced law in England as a young man. However, his Puritan leanings led him into the work to obtain a charter for the Massachusetts Bay Company, and he came to the foundling colony in 1630. It was his maneuvers, as much as or more than those of anyone else, which enabled the company to bring the charter to the New World. He served as governor of the colony for 13 years and as deputy-governor for 10 more. His journals were later published in two volumes as *The History of New England*.

Compact and the Fundamental Orders of Connecticut, the charters issued by kings, and the United States Constitution.

The leaders took seriously their belief that not only were they personally bound to live according to their understanding of God's ways but so also were all the inhabitants. Only church members in good standing could participate in the government. The government undertook to enforce morality upon all who lived in its jurisdiction. Both church members and others were expected to observe the Sabbath strictly and to avoid all vices. Churches were controlled by their members, but the state supported the church and enforced the moral code.

The Puritans were not tolerant of all persuasions or of any and every doctrine. Though they had themselves been dissenters sometimes in the past, there were limits to any they would countenance. They were not a debating society, as they understood it. When disagreement threatened the integrity of their communities, they were prepared to deal with it as harshly as might be needed. Their first step in dealing with those they judged to be making trouble was to banish them from the commonwealth. The worst trouble they had was with Quakers, who persisted in coming in, disturbing their worship, and denouncing them for their beliefs. When Quakers were expelled, they, or others, returned. Finally, their patience exhausted, the Puritans hanged several Quakers.

Not all those who came as Puritans were happy with arrangements in Massachusetts. Two other colonies were founded from such disagreements. One dissident was Thomas Hooker, who was pastor of the church at what is now Cambridge. He did not believe that church and state should be so closely related and, especially, that voting and government service should be reserved to church members. Hooker took such of his congregation as would go with him and moved southwest to found a settlement at Hartford in 1636. Several other groups left Massachusetts shortly to make settlements in Connecticut. In 1639, these settlers drew up and adopted the Fundamental Orders of Connecticut, which is often called the first written constitution in America. The town of New Haven was the location of a settlement at about the same time by a group of Puritans from England, led by John Davenport. Eventually, New Haven became a part of Connecticut.

The much more famous case of a dissident who founded a colony was that of Roger Williams. Williams was one of the early arrivals during the Puritan migration and became a popular pastor in the church at Salem. It did not take him long, however, before he was at odds with arrangements in Massachusetts. He did not believe that the Puritans had gone nearly far enough in purifying the church, opposed the use of government to enforce religion, and even questioned the legality of the charter. Probably, Williams had the sort of temperament that does not readily adjust to control by others. At any rate, Williams was expelled from Massachusetts, and founded the settlement of Providence in 1636.

Anne Hutchinson, a member of a Boston congregation, was an equally, or more, troublesome character than Roger Williams. Her fault, if fault it was, was to insist that the voice of God which spoke to a person individually must be heeded rather than the commands of either church or state. Since she had followers within her church and since such doctrine threatened the Puritan Commonwealth, she, too, was expelled from Massachusetts. She built some towns on Rhode Island, and these were joined to Providence by charter in 1663.

Some settlements were made in New Hampshire by Captain John Mason, but no large development occurred there in the earlier part of the colonial period. Sir Ferdinando Gorges had large plans for developing Maine as a feudal estate, but nothing came of his schemes. His heirs sold his claims to Massachusetts.

## *The Proprietary Colonies*

The initial colonies were founded by joint-stock companies. The model for these were the trading companies, such as the East Indian Company. The idea of the trading company was that it would be not so much an extensive settlement in some distant corner of the world as that Englishmen would establish coastal settlements to promote trade with the natives. The English settlements in the New World did not conform to the trading company pattern. In the first place, the Indians were not acclimated to extensive trade and were not easily induced to change their ways. In the second place, it became apparent early that only extensive settlements were likely to survive. It was impractical to have trading companies governing extensive colonies in America. And, in the third place, large scale migration of religious dissidents made trading a secondary factor in some of the colonies.

Viewed from the angle of English monarchy, though, the principal difficulty was that the colonies were slipping away from the English connection. The proprietary approach offered the possibility, at least, of linking colonies more closely to the monarch and tying them to the English system of government. The proprietary system was Medieval in character. The monarch granted extensive lands to a person of noble lineage. He might, then, govern in person or appoint someone to govern in his place. Since the lands were his usually, he could parcel them out as he chose and could, and most did, charge a quitrent to his tenants. This provided the proprietor an economic motive for seeing his grant develop.

In addition to New Hampshire and Maine, already discussed, the following were proprietary colonies in their inception:

## 1. Maryland

Maryland was granted to George Calvert, the first Lord Baltimore, in 1632. He died, however, at the time the charter was being prepared, and it was made in the name of his son, Cecilius Calvert, who became the second Lord Baltimore. The Calverts were Roman Catholics, and one of their purposes was to provide a refuge for Catholics in the New World. The Calverts were not only proprietors but also feudal lords, in effect. They were granted 10 million acres over which to rule. "The proprietor was empowered to subinfeudate his lands..., to set up manors,

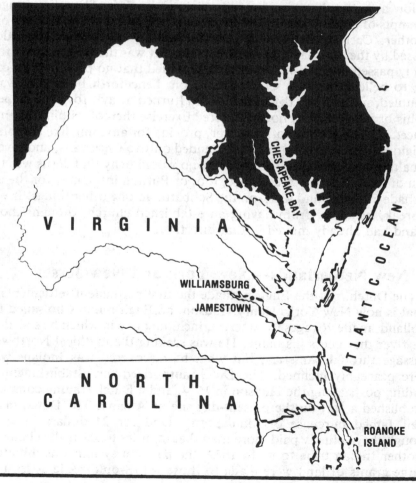

**Original Land Grant to Lord Baltimore**

with their manorial courts.... He was given the power to make laws, with the advice and consent of the freeholders, provided the laws made were not repugnant [contrary] to the laws of England.... He could collect rents and taxes from the land and make regulations governing the commerce of the colony.... In no other colony were the feudal institutions of landholding and society transplanted so completely to the soil of America."[18] There were a considerable number of large estates in Maryland from the outset, due to the manner of parceling out the land.

Although the Calverts hoped to make Maryland a refuge for Catholics, they did not expect that it would be settled by Catholics entirely, or even predominantly. From the very beginning, there were probably more Protestants than Catholics. There were not enough Catholics interested in coming to America to populate the land. Cecilius Calvert and his brother, Leonard, who became governor, attempted to follow a course that would avoid religious disputes. They discouraged attempts of either Catholics or Protestants to impose their views on one another. Cecilius Calvert succeeded in getting an Act of Toleration passed by the Maryland legislature in 1649. It was the first such act formally passed in English America. It provided that no person "professing to believe in Jesus Christ shall from henceforth be in any ways troubled, molested or discountenanced [turned away], for or in respect of his or her Religion, nor in the free Exercise thereof within this Province...." The act did not, however, provide for anything like complete religious liberty. Toleration was extended only to Christians, and severe penalties were provided for anyone who would deny that Jesus was the Son of God. There was evidence, too, of Puritan influence, for the act forbade swearing and work on the Sabbath, among other things. It was a break, however, from having an established church, though Rhode Island had already moved in that direction.

## 2. New Netherlands—New York and New Jersey

The Dutch, not the English, made the first permanent settlements in what is now New York. Henry Hudson, an Englishman who sailed for Holland, made voyages to America, including one in which he sailed up the river that bears his name. He was seeking the mythical Northwest Passage through America, but what he discovered was Indians who were peaceably inclined. The Dutch authorized the establishment of trading posts along the Hudson in 1614, and a Dutch trading company established a fort on the present-day site of Albany. The Dutch made their famed purchase of Manhattan Island for 24 dollars in 1626, though they actually paid more than that in order to settle the claims of another Indian tribe to it. In 1629, the patroon system was initiated. Large grants of land were made to those who would settle at least 50 adults in America. In consequence, a goodly number of landed Dutch families were established in America.

English rulers considered the Dutch as intruders in America, but little was done about it until 1664. In that year, King Charles II (1660-1685) granted a vast area, including parts of Connecticut, New York and New

## Henry Hudson (no dates)

Hudson was an English navigator and explorer, but he made some of his most important explorations for the Dutch. More than any other single explorer, his voyages were dominated by the effort to find a sea route to Asia. He made two voyages for the British Muscovy Company to find a polar passage to Asia by sailing northeast of Europe. Ice blocked his way on both occasions. In 1609, sailing for the Dutch, he explored the Hudson River, which was named for him, in a quest for a Northwest Passage through America. On a fourth voyage, this time for the English, he explored the Hudson Bay region. In the illustration above he is shown visiting with Indians along the Hudson River.

Jersey to the Duke of York. The only catch was that the Duke had to take it from the Dutch. This he proceeded to do in 1664. His charter was in most respects more generous in the grant of powers to him than those granted to the Lords Baltimore. The Duke of York was made sole proprietor and ruler of his vast domain. No provision was made for a legislature, and he was restricted only in that laws must be in accord with those in England and appeals could be made to the king from his decisions.

In practice, however, the Duke's government was not so severe as might have been expected. The Dutch were permitted to keep their property. Religious toleration was permitted. The territory that had been granted to the Duke of York in Connecticut was returned to that Puritan colony. New Jersey was separated from New York by the grant of that territory to John Lord Berkeley and Sir George Carteret.

## 3. The Carolinas

Although the charter for the settlement of Carolina, as the region comprising North and South Carolina, plus a portion of Georgia, was granted before the one for New York, it was several years before effective settlements were made. Charles II granted Carolina to eight proprietors, mostly noblemen. While the proprietors were granted the usual powers of appointing governors, the charter did give the rights of Englishmen to settlers and required that laws be made with the consent of the freemen. It was by this time getting to be much more difficult to lure settlers from England. To try to lure them, the proprietors promised generous terms of land distribution and religious toleration.

Even so, it was not easy to establish settlements. Settlers had moved into the Albemarle Sound region of North Carolina in the 1650s. More were drawn in after a governor was appointed for what was called

## Sir George Carteret
## (circa 1610-1680)

Carteret was one of the proprietors of the Carolinas, along with John Locke and John Lord Berkeley, and of New Jersey by a grant from the Duke of York in 1664. He was born on the Isle of Jersey in the British Isles, sided with the king during the English Civil War, and was somewhat of a court favorite after the Restoration in 1660. Carteret was not an active proprietor in the Carolinas, but he did take an active interest in the lands in New Jersey.

Albemarle County in the mid-1660s. This became the first permanent legitimate settlement in Carolina. A settlement was made at what became Charleston in South Carolina in 1670. Charleston flourished as a port, and the inhabitants prospered by the fur trade with the Indians, producing naval stores, and growing crops, such as rice, which were not grown further to the north. The two settlements were a great distance from one another, and the separation between North and South Carolina was recognized by the appointment of different governors in 1691. Their legislatures had always been distinct from one another.

## 4. Pennsylvania

Charles II granted the colony which became known as Pennsylvania to William Penn in 1681. The next year the Duke of York ceded Delaware to Penn. There had been several settlements in the Penn colonies long before he acquired them. The Dutch, Swedes, Danes, and some Puritans from New Haven had planted settlements within the bounds. By the grants made to him, Penn became proprietor of these colonies, had the authority to govern, and was empowered to make laws with the consent of the freemen. The charter did, however, restrict the proprietor by requiring that laws be in accord with English law, providing for appeals to England from courts in Pennsylvania, and specifying that Parliament might make laws which would apply to the colonies. Freedom of worship for members of the Church of England was also protected in the charter.

William Penn was a Quaker, a follower of George Fox. The Quakers, or Society of Friends, were an offshoot of the Puritan movement in England. They differed from most Puritans, as well as other Christian churches, however, in that they had no specific creed or set of beliefs to which they subscribed, no professional clergy, no sacraments and no liturgy. Their emphasis was upon the inward rather than the outward aspects of Christianity. They emphasized the illumination of an Inner Light, God within man, and the importance of personal conversion. In their view, outward forms of religion are largely meaningless. They have generally been pacifists, and their opposition to the use of force has often been so thorough that they have sometimes doubted that they ought to participate in government at all.

The Quakers were persecuted in England, especially from 1660 to 1689: for holding meetings in defiance of the law, for refusing to take oaths, and for failure to support the established church. They came in considerable numbers to various colonies in America, but they were welcome only in Rhode Island until the founding of New Jersey. Penn conceived his colonies not only as a refuge for Quakers but also a place where any who sought to live peaceably and were persecuted might come. The law in Pennsylvania provided that "all persons...who con-

# William Penn
## (1644-1718)

Penn was born in London of a prominent English family. At about the age of 22 he was converted to the Quaker faith and devoted much time to spreading his beliefs. He suffered persecution himself (was expelled from Oxford earlier for his Puritan beliefs and imprisoned for Quaker activities) and, when the occasion offered, was eager to provide a refuge for those persecuted for their religion. Penn applied to Charles II for a grant of land as settlement of a debt owed to the Penn family by the king, and it was granted in 1681. Pennsylvania (Penn's Woods) was named for him.

fess and acknowledge the one Almighty and eternal God...and that hold themselves obliged in conscience to live peacefully and justly in civil society, shall, in no ways, be molested or prejudiced for their religious persuasion..., nor shall they be compelled, at any time, to frequent or maintain any religions worship.'' Pennsylvania came as near to religious liberty as any colony ever did in the colonial period. It always provided, too, for popular election of the legislature, though there were several changes in the form of the government.

## 5. Georgia

Georgia differed from the other colonies not only in that it was the last one founded but also because it was founded for philanthropic purposes, so far as the founders were concerned. That is, those who started the settlement and oversaw it for 20 years did not do so for profit. In 1732, the Crown conferred on 21 trustees proprietary powers over Georgia. General Edward Oglethorpe was the leader among the trustees and also came to Georgia to direct the enterprise. Oglethorpe was greatly concerned with the conditions in British prisons, the fate of those who were sent to prison for failure to pay their debts, and with what happened to them once they were released. The British government was interested in establishing a buffer state between Spanish Florida and South Carolina. There was also interest in developing products which could be grown in more southerly climates.

The philanthropic experiment in Georgia was a failure. The trustees lost interest in the colony before the 21 years alloted them in the charter ran out. Parliament had repeatedly subsidized the undertaking, but when it refused to do so again in 1751, the trustees took action to surrender the charter voluntarily. Thus, Georgia became a Crown colony in 1752. From 1733 to 1751 about 5,000 people had settled in Georgia. In 1751 there were only about 3,000 inhabitants. This decline in population could not be ascribed to any great epidemic, Indian massacre, or the harshness of the climate. Instead, it can be explained mainly by the fact that many were dissatisfied and moved elsewhere.

The experiment in Georgia failed mainly because what the trustees, and especially General Oglethorpe, thought would be good for the inhabitants differed from what many of the settlers there wanted. The trustees wanted to settle the people in a town they built at Savannah and to limit their land holdings. The lands were entailed, also, that is, they could not be sold and had to be passed on to the eldest son in the family. The first settlers were required to plant mulberry trees for silk worms, in the expectation that the colony would produce silk. Strong drink and slavery were prohibited. In addition, men often had to be away from their work to serve as soldiers. Moreover, for most of the period the inhabitants had no say in the government, for there was no elected legislature. Although the trustees modified some of these provisions over the years, many people left for South Carolina where they could follow their own bent.

Even so, Georgia had been established as a colony by 1752.

# Chapter 5
# The Development and Growth of the Colonies

*January 27, 1711 I rose at 5 o'clock and read two chapters in Hebrew and some Greek in Lucian. I said my prayers and ate boiled milk for breakfast. I danced my dance. It rained all night but held up about 8 o'clock this morning. My sick people were all better, thank God Almighty. I settled several accounts; then I read some English which gave me great light into the nature of spirit.... In the afternoon my wife and I took a little walk and then danced together. Then I read some more English. At night I read some Italian and then played at Piquet with my wife.... I said my prayers and had good health, good thoughts, and good humor, thank God Almighty.*

—*The Secret Diary of William Byrd of Westover*, **1711**

## Chronology

1662—Half-Way Covenant.

1663—Maryland Statute Establishes Negro Slavery.

1675—King Philip's War.

1676—Bacon's Rebellion.

1685—Revocation of Edict of Nantes.

1686—Dominion of New England.

1692—Salem Witchcraft Trials.

1706—Presbyterian Church Organized in Philadelphia.

1710—German Migration to Pennsylvania.

1714—Beginning of Scots-Irish Migration to America.

1730s—The Great Awakening.

American colonial history lacks the kind of unity which makes for a coherent and easily followed narrative. The colonies were not politically, economically, socially or religiously linked to one another for most of the long colonial period. Even the physical connections were limited until well into the 18th century. Colonies were usually planted near some natural harbor or on a navigable river. Overland travel by road only developed slowly, and it was hampered by the location of settlements at the wide parts of rivers which were rarely, if ever, bridged. A postal system was established in the 1690s, but it was not very effective until Benjamin Franklin imparted energy to it in the 1750s.

The colonies could be considered as linked together as a part of a British empire. But that is not very helpful either. Though there were political links between particular colonies and England, the differences in the way these were maintained were often more pronounced than the similarities. The colonies were never governed from England, except for brief intervals, and even at these intervals the effort was not consolidated. James II, whose short rule occurred in the late 1680s, did have a plan for bringing the colonies under much closer British supervision. He planned to set up three dominions in eastern America, and thus to tighten British rule. He never got any further along with this, however, than setting up the Dominion of New England in 1686 under Sir Edmund Andros. This move met with such strong resistance that it was abandoned. It is unlikely that it would have succeeded much better elsewhere.

Even the colonies chosen for study is something decided after the fact. First and last there were other British colonies in America that are ordinarily given little or no attention in the background to the United States. That is mainly because, as in the case of Canada, they did not become member states of the United States. Thus, it was only after 1776 that it could have been known which colonies would be most important for American history.

What gives these separate and distinct colonies unity for us, then, is that they eventually became part of a union. However great the differences between Puritan Massachusetts and colonial Virginia or Quaker Pennsylvania and plantation-dominated South Carolina, they were eventually sufficiently narrowed for these colonies to become states in the United States. One point on which to focus is how the differences were becoming less, or how they were being drawn closer together by common experiences. Another theme that unites the colonies is that of how Englishmen transplanted in the New World were becoming Americans. A counter theme, of equal importance, is the preservation of their English heritage and the vital connections they maintained with European civilization. These unifying themes can be emphasized without losing sight of the ways in which colonies continued to differ from one another. After all, their differences are as necessary to understanding the system Americans instituted once they were separated from England as are the things that linked them to one another to the fact that they joined together to make the separation. Both the diversity and unity are critical aspects of American history throughout.

## Population Growth and Movement

One of the great changes during the colonial period was the great growth in population. Some figures will indicate the extent of the change. (Indians were rarely counted in the population figures or estimates.) There were approximately 5,000 settlers living in America in 1630; 50,368 in 1650; 250,888 in 1700; 629,000 in 1730, and 1,170,760 in 1750. Except for the very early years, there was steady and continued growth in the population of all the colonies. However, there were great differences in population from colony to colony. Virginia had the largest population of any colony throughout the colonial period. But once the Puritan migration to Massachusetts Bay had taken place, Massachusetts had nearly as many people as Virginia for many years. For example, in 1650 Virginia had 18,731 residents and Massachusetts 16,603; in 1700 Virginia had 58,560 and Massachusetts 55,941. However, by 1770 Virginia had 447,016 compared to 235,308 for Massachusetts. By contrast, South Carolina had only 64,000 as late as 1750, New Hampshire 27,505 and Georgia 5,200.

The growth in population not only signified the success of English colonization but much else besides. By 1650 the larger settlements were not only well established but outnumbered any challengers in the vicinity. By 1730 there were as many or more people in the English colonies as there were Indians east of the Rockies. By 1770, when there were over 2 million inhabitants, the population of English America was less than half that of Great Britain, but it was sufficiently large to make the combined colonies a potential force in the world. America was no longer simply an appendage of Europe, if it had ever been.

Much of the increase in population was due to the excess of births over deaths. Up to 1689 most of the settlers in English America came from England. Further, as Clinton Rossiter said, "Although immigration from England tapered off sharply after 1689, the high rate of natural increase among the early families of New England and the tidewater had... [toward the end of the colonial period] produced a basic stock of perhaps one million English-Americans. It was these people, of course, who controlled America—politically, linguistically, culturally, and institutionally."[19] The first actual census of the population in America was made in 1790. A much later scholarly analysis of that census concluded that the white population was composed of the following national stocks: "English 60.9, Scotch 8.3, Ulster Irish [probably mostly Scotch-Irish] 6, Free State Irish 3.7, German 8.7, Dutch 3.4, French 1.7, unassigned 6.6."[20]

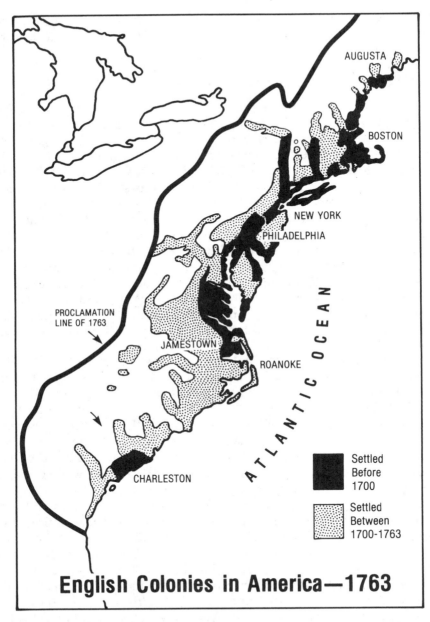

**English Colonies in America—1763**

Except for the English, Dutch and Swedes, most of the other nationalities had migrated to America in the late 17th and first half of the 18th centuries. The French came to America in considerable numbers during the decade or so after Louis XIV revoked the Edict of Nantes. Under this edict French Protestants had been tolerated. They were mostly Huguenots (Calvinists) and lived in towns and cities in France.

THE DEVELOPMENT AND GROWTH OF THE COLONIES

Some of the Huguenots attempted to settle in New England, but despite the fact that their religious beliefs were similar to those of the Puritans, they did not get along well there. Important settlements were made in New York state, and from these centers they moved into Pennsylvania and New Jersey. The greatest concentration of French immigrants, however, was in South Carolina. There, they were sufficiently numerous to become an important element among the planters and in Charleston society.

German immigration to America became important after 1700. The main cause of the German migration was religious persecution. Ever since the onset of the Reformation, there had been several sects, called Pietists in general, in Germany. There were Moravians, Mennonites, Dunkards and so on. They were often subject to persecution both by the large Protestant denominations—Lutherans and Calvinists—and Roman Catholics. But it was Catholic persecution in the Palitinate of Germany that drove many of them to migrate in the early 18th century. Several thousand were located in the New York colony, but they were subjected to land discrimination there. Some of these eventually made their way to east central Pennsylvania. Their treatment in Pennsylvania was so superior to that elsewhere that German settlers came mainly to that colony thereafter. These are the people known as "Pennsylvania Dutch." So numerous were they that in 1766 Benjamin Franklin estimated that people of German ancestry made up one-third of the population of Pennsylvania.

The migration from Ireland to America in the colonial period was even greater than that from Germany. The Irish immigrants can be classified as the Celtic-Irish and the Scots-Irish. The Celtic-Irish were probably Catholic and came mostly as servants. They did not come in groups but as individuals and families. In consequence, except for such of the Irish names that survived, they became indistinguishable from the English inhabitants. By contrast, many of the Scots-Irish came in waves. The first great migration occurred between 1714 and 1720, when more than a hundred ship loads of them landed in New England, Maryland, Delaware and South Carolina. The Scots-Irish were Presbyterians, Scottish in ancestry, whose ancestors had been encouraged to migrate to Ulster in Ireland in the early 17th century. The English gave many families 99-year leases to induce them to move. These leases ran out in the early 17th century, were not renewed generally, and many families came to America. Scots came in considerable numbers, too, nearer the middle of the 18th century. They were mostly Highlanders, whose clans were broken up by the English government after rebellions in 1715 and 1745.

These non-English immigrants, particularly the Germans, Scots-Irish and Scots, contributed much to the settlement of the back country in the English colonies. The English settlers, as already noted, settled around the rivers near the coast of eastern America. Nor were they inclined to move further back than 50 to 100 miles during the whole of the colonial epoch. Later settlers often moved into the back country because land was more readily acquired there and it was much easier to maintain their distinctive ways separate from the older settlers. Too, the Germans, Scots-Irish and Scots were mostly farmers and continued that vocation in America. The Germans settled in such south central counties in Pennsylvania as Lancaster, Berks and Montgomery. The Scots-Irish and Scots were more adventurous than the Germans, less concerned with settling in communities, and by background drawn to the hills and mountains even farther to the west. Some settled in the back county of New York, many in Pennsylvania, while others moved southwestward into western Maryland, the Shenandoah Valley of Virginia, into the western Carolinas, and eventually across the mountains into what are now West Virginia, Kentucky and Tennessee.

However, the largest influx of newcomers, aside from the English, to the colonies has not yet been mentioned. That was the Negroes brought in from Africa. They did not come voluntarily, of course; instead, they were brought in bondage to the New World. Black Africans were captured by other black Africans—slave hunters or catchers—who brought them to the coast to trade for goods with European shipmasters. "Then came the horrors of the 'middle passage' to America. The hapless passengers were herded like cattle in unsanitary ships where many perished because of inadequate ventilation, food, and water."[21] They were taken to the West Indies where they were broken and given a period of training. Only then, were such as were left brought to the mainland, transported there for sale at auctions.

A Dutch ship brought the first Negroes to English America in 1619. Thereafter, for the next 30 or 40 years occasional shiploads were brought to one colony or another. Slavery was unknown to English law, nor did the colonists rush to pass any laws. The nearest thing to it was indentured servitude. Indentured servants were bound by contract to serve some master, or masters, for a specific length of time. At the end of the period, they were usually freed, if that was their desire, and often provided by the master with the means of getting a living. There is a theory, advanced by some historians, that the Negroes brought in during the first half of the 17th century were treated as indentured servants. Apparently, some were freed, but the evidence is too scanty for drawing any general conclusions. What is clear is that in the second half of the century recognizable slavery had taken hold supported by law in the colonies. A Maryland law provided in 1663 that all Negroes could be held in bondage for life and that children of slaves inherited the status. The slave "had no resort to the courts; his offspring were subjected to

NORTH AMERICA
IN 1700

NORTH AMERICA
AFTER 1713

NORTH AMERICA
AFTER 1763

FRENCH          ENGLISH

RUSSIAN         SPANISH

perpetual bondage; his mobility was restricted to the general jurisdiction of his master; runaways were severely punished; and even minor crimes by slaves were dealt with harshly.''²² Slavery was general throughout the colonies, and there was probably little difference from one to another in how they could be treated. For example, a law in Pennsylvania passed in 1693 authorized any citizens ''to take up Negroes, male or female, whom they shall find gadding abroad on the first days of the week without a ticket from their master or mistress..., to take them to jail, there to remain that night, and that without meat or drink, and to cause them to be publicly whipped next morning with 39 lashes, well laid on their backs, at which their said master or mistress shall pay 15 pence to the whipper.'' Quaker humanitarianism apparently did not modify at law the treatment of slaves.

In the latter half of the colonial period, British and New England shippers brought most of the slaves into the colonies. In 1672, the British chartered the Royal African Company and gave it a monopoly of the slave trade. However, it was only after the Treaty of Utrecht of 1713, which permitted the British to bring slaves to the Spanish colonies, that the British became really active in the slave trade. But no company actually monopolized the trade, for it was much too profitable for shippers to give it up, whether they were authorized to engage in it or not. Rhode Islanders, out of Newport, were the most active New Englanders in the trade. It should be pointed out, however, that many Southern planters were deeply involved in the slave trade, at least on the buying end.

Although slavery existed in all the colonies, it was increasingly concentrated in the colonies south of Pennsylvania from the late 17th century onward. The essential difference was that slavery never became integral to the Northern economy as it did in the South. Southern farms grew most of the crops—tobacco, rice and indigo—which were important in international trade. These crops were not only profitable, providing the means for buying slaves, but were also well adapted to the use of slaves on a large scale. The largest number of slaves were in Virginia and South Carolina.

## *Towns, Plantations and Farms*

In western Europe, farmers usually live in villages. In the United States, farmers customarily live in houses separated by some distance, if not isolated, from one another. This difference between Europe and America began to occur early in the colonial period and tended to widen over the years. The most direct explanation of the change is in land distribution and the size of land holdings. European farmers often have only a few acres of land, and they are easily reached from the village. By contrast, American farms have been much larger than that. Even the smallest farms here have almost always consisted of at least 40 acres, and farms of several hundred acres have been common in most places from the outset. When farms are that large, it is much more practical to live in the midst of the farm, or else too much time would be consumed going back and forth from house to land.

There was, however, a major effort made to establish the village or town system, somewhat on the European model, in New England. Not only were the Puritans themselves mostly townspeople and influenced by the English pattern, but also they conceived it as a means of maintaining political and religious control over the development of colonies. The companies, or governments of the colonies, achieved their aim of having settlements made in towns by granting blocks of land to towns. The lands were then parceled out to families, usually in small lots. They intended to found farming communities with lands that could be farmed by inhabitants of the towns. How closely these towns resembled one another is suggested by an historian of the settlements. "Throughout this entire section," he said, "the study of local settlement and of town government is the study of a single model and of the somewhat minute variations to which...it was subjected. Local settlements in the section preferred to conform as strictly to a single type as do the colonies themselves."[23]

The governments of the colonies could do much of their governing by laying down rules for the towns. They could, for example, require the towns to provide schools. They could make them responsible for poor relief. Each town, too, had one church, and only one usually. The bounds of a congregation, then, were the same as those of a town. That made it much easier and simpler for the close ties between church and state to be maintained than would otherwise have been the case.

South of New England, land grants were usually much larger than those in New England after the early years. The Dutch Patroon system, already discussed, assured large landholdings in New York from the outset. After the English took over, many large grants of land were still made. In the Penn colonies, William Penn offered 500 acres initially to any family that would settle there. Though the size of the grants was generally reduced later, middle-sized farms were common. In the Southern colonies, the headright system was widely employed. In Virginia, the usual practice was to grant 50 acres per person settled on the land. The grants were made to the person undertaking the settlement; thus, it was possible to put together large holdings by bringing in many servants.

As a result of the size of the farms, except in New England, farmers usually did not live in villages and towns. Instead, they lived amidst their land, separate from one another. There can be little doubt that this fostered a spirit of self-reliance, close families, independence, and what is often called individualism. To this day, Americans favor detached houses set amidst as much land as they can afford. Many who have gone to the cities to work still cherish the dream of owning their own acreage with a house located on it. The pattern for this was set in the colonial period.

In the South the word "plantation" took on a new meaning. It became a settlement on a large farm owned by one family. The settlement consisted of the large family dwelling, the slave cabins, barns, smokehouses, blacksmith shops and other supporting dwellings and buildings. In Virginia, where such plantations became widespread, no towns of any size developed in the colonial period. As one writer has noted, "From a commercial point of view...cities were superfluous. The tobacco grower could load his hogsheads directly from his own dockside onto the ship which went to his agent in London; his imports could be landed at his private port-of-entry."[24] In a sense, plantations were villages or towns themselves. Their model, so far as there was one in Europe, was the medieval manor.

Even so, some large towns, budding cities, did develop during the colonial period. They were all port cities. From the outset, almost, Boston was the largest of these towns. In 1730 Boston had about 13,000 inhabitants, compared to 11,500 for Philadelphia, 8,500 for New York City. Charleston, too, was an important port town in South Carolina. Philadelphia had grown to be the largest city by the end of the colonial period, followed by New York, then Boston. These cities were not only commercial centers in their region but also cultural centers. They were large enough to have newspapers, publishing houses and book stores. Although Virginians might argue the point, the connection between city and civilization is not simply verbal. Towns played a vital role in the transplantation of European civilization to the New World.

## *The Disintegration of Class System*

America has never had a full-fledged class system, neither when it was English America nor the United States. It has had relics of European classes, has had at least one underclass fixed over a period of two centuries at law, has had some developments from time to time in the direction of establishing classes, and has had at all times distinctions among people which received support within the society. But it has never had a full-fledged class system, such as existed in England or France, say, in the Middle Ages. A full-fledged class system is one in which class status is hereditary, is based on privileges at law, is maintained and supported by government, and in which change in status is most difficult to achieve. Even England did not have such a firmly fixed class system as that as far back as the beginning of the 17th century.

There were some sporadic attempts to transplant the English class system in America. Monarchs bestirred themselves on occasion in that direction: by appointing governors of aristocratic station and by granting lands to proprietors of noble ancestry, for example. But they never succeeded in exporting any considerable number of English nobility to America. There is a saying that "Dukes don't migrate," and it worked out that way in America. Most of those of noble lineage who came to America stayed for only a brief period and then returned to England. Therefore, there was no upper class in America, in the British sense.

Colonial governments tried, too, in the early years to maintain the distinctions that existed in England. Those who came over were used to all sorts of distinctions, vouchsafed by titles, such as squire, master, mister, mistress, goodman, goodwoman, and the like. Those who valued the privileges attached to these various stations sought to maintain them. For example, an act passed in Massachusetts in 1651 stated:

> We declare our utter detestation and dislike that men and women of mean condition should take upon themselves the garb of gentlemen, by wearing of gold or silver lace or buttons, or points at their knees, or to walk in boots, or women of the same rank to wear silk or tiffany...scarfs, which though allowable to persons of greater estate, or more liberal education, yet we cannot but judge it intolerable in persons of such like condition.

In 1674 a tailor was punished in Virginia for horse racing, because the court held that "it was contrary to law for a labourer to make a race, being a sport only for gentlemen."

These were mostly holding actions, however, for there is little doubt that the class system disintegrated in America. By the time of the adoption of the United States Constitution, there were spokesmen for the view that classes had no standing in this country. Edmund Pendleton, in the Virginia Convention, took exception to the words of a speaker who alluded to class distinctions. He said:

> I am unfortunate enough to differ from the worthy member in another circumstance. He professes himself an advocate for the middling and lower classes of men. I profess to be a friend to the equal liberty of all men, from the palace to the cottage without any other distinction than that between good and bad men....
>
> Why bring into the debate the whims of writers—introducing the distinction of *well-born* from others? I consider every man well-born who comes into the world with an intelligent mind, and with all his parts perfect.[25]

R.R. Livingston, speaking in the New York debates, declared: "The truth is, in these republican governments, we know no such ideal distinctions. We are all equally aristocrats. Offices, emoluments [pay], honors, are open to all."[26]

That might well be, but is was customary then, as now, to make some distinctions among people based on their station in life. Some were reckoned to be higher, others lower. But a major change had occurred in America in the basis of classifications. In the course of the colonial period the basis had shifted away from royalty granted privileges, legally maintained classes, and heredity toward merit and personal attainments. It was no longer one's rank in the courts of monarchs that counted for much but rather what one had achieved by his own efforts. There were still elements of heredity intermingled with standing, but they were no longer determinative in most instances. America was already becoming a land of opportunity, and opportunity meant precisely the possibility of improving oneself by effort and achievement.

Professor Clinton Rossiter referred to the distinctions that arose in colonial America as being between the "Better Sort," "Middling Sort," and "Meaner Sort." They may not be very precise, but that is an advantage. The distinctions were largely informal rather than legalistic, and that is the way they should be described.

The "Better Sort" consisted of men of wealth and standing in their communities, of large landholders or planters, of prosperous merchants, or of other noteworthy attainments. Some few of them were descendants of the English gentry, but more often they had risen to their standing through their own efforts in America. There was nothing formal or legal about their standing, as a rule. What distinguished them, above all, was a style of life, the means to maintain it, and a view of their duties and obligations. Above all, they aspired to be gentlemen. That this was not a legal category, even in England, was well illustrated by the answer of King James I when his nurse asked him to make her son a gentleman. "A gentleman I could never make him," he said, "though I could make him a lord."[27] The ideal of the gentleman had taken shape in the Renaissance; it was the modern counterpart to the medieval ideal of knighthood. The knight was a warrior, however; whereas, the gentleman was a man of affairs of diverse attainments. It was the dream of middle class Englishmen, says Daniel Boorstin, and in that country it meant having a spacious "manor house in the midst of broad acres.... But it was more than that; becoming a country gentleman in those days meant joining the governing class. To acquire a manor house meant also to become a justice of the peace, a power over the local pulpit, a patron and father-confessor to the local peasantry, an overseer of the poor, and perhaps sooner or later a member of Parliament."[28]

While the American ideal of a gentleman bore a family resemblance to the English model, it was adjusted to American circumstances. One way to describe those of the "Better Sort" or gentlemen is to say that they had reached a financial position where they did not have to do physical labor for a living. This was not necessarily an aversion to such work; rather, it freed them from the necessity for specialization and enabled them to develop their talents in many directions. William Byrd II, of Westover, was an outstanding example of a Virginia gentleman. Byrd inherited over 20,000 acres from his father and put together an estate of 179,400 acres. He lived amidst this vast estate in a mansion he called Westover. He served as a member of the governor's council, a vestryman in the Anglican Church, oversaw his vast estate, and kept abreast of affairs in England and America. Byrd could read several foreign languages, including Latin and Greek, put together a library of several hundred volumes, kept a diary in his almost indecipherable shorthand, and wrote two important books.

A gentleman might be a planter, a shipper, a merchant, a physician, a lawyer, a printer, but he was most often a man of large and varied interests who saw it as his duty to develop his many talents. In 18th century America, there were an increasing number of such men: the Carters, Lees and Randolphs of Virginia; the Rutledges and Pinckneys of South Carolina; the Carrolls of Maryland, and the Winthrops, Saltonstalls and Dudleys of Massachusetts. This ideal of the multi-

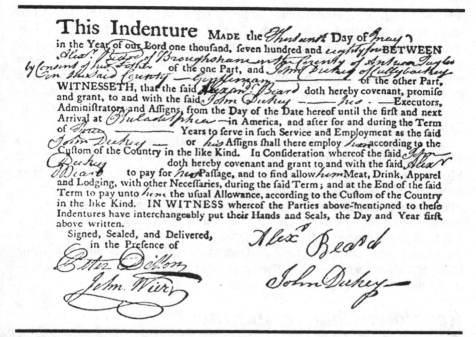

**An Eighteenth Century Indenture Contract.** *Dated May 13, 1784, this contract was made late in the history of indentured servitude and is typical of the standardized form that developed. Notice that it is a printed form with spaces left blank to be filled in.*

talented gentleman reached its epitome in such men as Thomas Jefferson, Benjamin Franklin, John Adams and George Washington. They were central figures in the making of the American republic.

The "Middling Sort" were more likely to be farmers than anything else. Indeed, most Americans were farmers in colonial America. The "Middling Sort" of farmer was one who has enough land to be independent, made an adequate to good living for his family, might or might not have a few servants or slaves, and worked on his own lands. Such people were called yeoman farmers both in England and America. The "Middling Sort" also included other occupations as well, any in which a man worked under his own direction, was independent, and made an adequate living. The category included carpenters, masons, tailors, cabinetmakers and skilled tradesmen of all sorts.

The "Meaner Sort" consisted of all those who worked under the direction and control of others and were dependent upon them for a livelihood. They were renters of land, day laborers, sailors and servants of one kind or another. They were not "mean" necessarily in a moral sense but rather "demeaned" by their dependence upon and servitude to others.

The largest number in this category who were of European descent were indentured servants. Since indentured servants were only bound to serve for a specified number of years, it was a temporary status. For many, indentured servitude was a way to get passage to America. They sold themselves to a ship's captain, or others interested in bringing them to America, and were bought by those who would be their masters in this country. For the young, it might be a way to learn a trade. At the end of their indenture, they might then move into a more nearly independent station, as farmers, laborers or craftsmen.

The lowest of the demeaned positions was that of slavery. This was so ordinarily because they rarely were freed in the course of their lives. More, they were devoid of rights or protections at law. There were laws protecting indentured servants, but few, if any, for slaves. Even so, there were better and worse positions for slaves. Generally speaking, it was much better to be a house servant than a field hand. It was better to work in the tobacco fields of Virginia than the rice swamps of South Carolina. Some slaves became craftsmen, thereby increasing their value to their master, and perhaps their standing. But slavery was demeaning to all who were caught in it.

## Religious Change and the Great Awakening

In the course of the colonial period religion was becoming less and less a divisive factor among the colonists. That is not to say that differences about doctrine, ritual and church organizations did not continue to exist. Moreover, it would be possible to focus on and highlight these differences so as to make them appear to be an uncrossable barrier to any eventual union. But they were not, and this was mainly the result of changes that occurred during the colonial period. For one thing, the idea and practice of religious tolerance was spreading. For another, rigorous attachment to doctrines was losing favor. Opposition to established churches was gaining ground, along with the idea of freedom of conscience.

Before describing the ways in which they were lessened, however, it may be helpful to note some of the basic differences in the religious faiths of the colonists. The greatest difference was between Protestants and Catholics. Since Catholics were not numerous generally, and since even in the colonies where they were more numerous they were in the minority, this was not a difference which divided the colonies. In terms of doctrine, the major differences were between Calvinists, Pietists and what, for want of a better term, may be called Latitudinarians. Calvinists emphasized God's sovereignty, the primacy of the Scriptures and belief in precise doctrines. Pietists emphasized inward faith and outward morality. The Church of England (and in its own way, the

Roman Catholic Church) was Latitudinarian. That is, it allowed for much latitude of belief in matters of doctrine.

In church organization (polity), there were three main divisions: congregational, presbyterian, and episcopal. Congregational churches are those in which the congregation (members) make the basic decisions in governing the church. Among those organized on the congregation pattern were: the Congregational churches of New England (Puritans derived from Calvinism), Baptists, Quakers, Moravians and so on. Presbyterian churches are organized into groups as presbyteries, and the ministers play a dominant role in governing them. The Presbyterian church (Scots-Calvinist in origin) was the only significant church in colonial America governed in this fashion. Episcopal churches are ruled by bishops. The Church of England was the largest of these, but the Roman Catholic and Lutheran churches are also episcopal in organization.

Politically, the most important division was between the churchly denominations and the sectarians. Churchly denominations are those which believe in or have an established church, that is, have close connections with government and are maintained by it. Among those denominations with a churchly bent in colonial America were the Congregationalists, Church of England, Catholic and Presbyterian. The Congregational church was established in Massachusetts, Connecticut and New Hampshire. The Church of England was, at one time or another, established, in varying degrees, in Virginia, the Carolinas, New York, Maryland and Georgia. It was only strongly supported, however, in Virginia and South Carolina, and only in Virginia was it fully established. Sectarians were those which neither had, wanted, nor believed in an established church. Among the sects were the Baptists, Quakers and Mennonites.

The sectarians were at the forefront of religious toleration and ultimately, religious freedom. The first of the sectarians to hold power was Roger Williams in Rhode Island. Williams denied that there could be any good effect to enforced religion. God chose whom He would for salvation and rejected the others; no good works or any other human agency or action could affect God's choice. Both the saved and the damned must live in society with one another, and government was necessary to that end. But it would be an abomination to attempt to enforce the dictates of religion on those not chosen; it would disturb the peace of the community, give decision over religious matters to unqualified men in government, and would dangerously intertwine matters of this world and the next. Thus, he favored toleration. So did William Penn, and the Quaker colonies tolerated all denominations.

Two other developments promoted religious toleration in the colonies over the years. One was that several of the colonies had numerous settlers with differing religious backgrounds. In those circumstances, it was often too much trouble for the authorities to enforce religious conformity. The Maryland Act of Toleration was born of conditions like that. Sectarians became numerous in the back country of such colonies as North Carolina, and that worked against the established religion.

The other development was the neglect of the colonies by the Church of England. No Anglican bishop ever came to or resided in the American colonies. Thus, the Church of England had no head in America. The Bishop of London was placed in charge of the American colonies. He sometimes appointed commissaries, as they were called, to act for him. The best known of these were Thomas Bray in Maryland and James Blair in Virginia. But these men could not ordain ministers nor confirm church members. There was such a shortage of ministers that the establishment in some colonies existed in name only, and in others people in the back country were neglected. This neglect not only resulted in the Americanization of the Anglican church but also permitted other denominations to grow undisturbed in some of the colonies.

The narrowing of the gap between denominations was assisted, too, by the common Christian heritage they shared. After all, virtually all the inhabitants of English America of European descent were Christians, nominally, habitually or devoutly. As Christians, they accepted God as Creator, Provider and Disposer. Life they viewed within a framework of Time and Eternity. Time was that dimension within which man lived out his alloted years; a span fraught with ultimate significance, for it was then that the decision for Eternity was made. To be a Christian has meant, to say the least, the acceptance of the entering of God more directly into history through Jesus Christ, the providing of a way of salvation through His grace, and the setting in motion of events which will culminate with His return. All Christians agree, too, that the Bible is the basic source of information about these things.

Moreover, most Christians were Protestants in the colonies. Not only did they share the Reformation heritage but also many common practices. For example, they accepted married clergymen and rejected monasticism. That is, Protestants do not accept a priesthood or orders of men and women (as monks and nuns) set apart from the ways of the world and consecrated to the religious life. Rather, Protestants have generally held that all Christians should be involved with the tasks of this world, however dangerous this might be to the state of their souls.

This thinking resulted in an attitude toward worldly endeavors among Protestants in many ways distinct from that of Roman Catholics. This attitude is sometimes referred to as the Puritan ethic, but it was actually shared in greater or lesser degrees by most Protestants. For one thing, Protestants generally abandoned the practice of a clergy set apart from the world. For another, English Protestants were

## Thomas Bray
## (1656-1730)

Bray was a minister in the Church of England who was sent to Maryland as commissary for the Bishop of London to organize churches there. Though he did not stay long, nor greatly advance the Anglican Church, he retained a long-term interest in promoting libraries in the colonies. The original idea was to provide books for parish libraries, but it was soon expanded to include the founding of public libraries. The library he helped to found at Annapolis soon had 1,000 volumes. The public library movement in America owed much to Bray.

generally greatly influenced by Puritanism (or Calvinism). The Church of England was influenced, if in no other way, by the large number of Puritans who were in it from time to time. Rhode Island Baptists were obviously influenced by Calvinism. Though to a lesser extent, so were the Quakers. Thus, if Puritanism were the center of the Protestant ethic, it would still have spread to the others.

In this ethic, there is a somewhat ambiguous attitude toward life in the world. To devout Protestants generally, the things of the world are a snare and a delusion. Yet, they are called to grapple with them, possess them, and keep them in their proper perspective—i.e., as things to be used rather than to be used by them. The particular posture of this ethic toward the workaday world is most clearly seen in the Puritan Doctrine of the Calling. According to this doctrine, God calls to useful employment all whom he elects to salvation. This calling may be any lawful undertaking by which he may support himself and those dependent upon him and which serves others generally. This doctrine promoted much zeal in the performance of work, for a man showed forth the character of his faith by the quality of his work.

For Protestants, personal piety tended to replace the special devotions of the religious among Roman Catholics. Piety is a vesting of all things and all acceptable activities with religious significance, a significance that derives from their impact on the souls of persons involved with them. Anything that cannot be done to the glory of God cannot be rightfully done. One of the outreaches of these beliefs was the vigorous trade and productive activities, so characteristic of America for much of its history. It is true, no doubt, that people generally are moved to produce in the hope of gain. But they are also given to lethargy, wastefulness, and carelessness. The Protestant ethic provided an important counterweight to these tendencies.

The Great Awakening was the first religious development to have an impact throughout the colonies. And, since it did, many who felt its effects shared a common religious experience. The Great Awakening was a revival movement, the first one in America, which swept up and down the coast of English America and into the back country in the 1730s and 1740s. Jonathan Edwards, a man of great learning, a deep thinker, and a fiery evangelist (though he spoke quietly), was the leader in New England. George Whitefield, an English evangelist, held meetings in many colonies and moved many to repentance and conversion. Gilbert Tennent led the revival among Presbyterians in the Middle Colonies. It was through this movement that evangelical piety began its move to become the dominant way of American religion.

### Jonathan Edwards
### (1703-1758)

Edwards was born in Connecticut, trained at Yale, became a Congregational minister, and was pastor of churches in New York and Massachusetts. He was the leading Calvinist thinker in 18th century America, sparked the Great Awakening in New England, and was a foremost philosopher of his time. In his later years, he became a missionary to the Indians, and in the last year of his life accepted an appointment as President of the College of New Jersey (Princeton).

The evangelical movement took the emphasis away from doctrine, from forms and ritual, and from what, in more general terms, may be called "churchiness." What was essential was not outward conformity to religious forms but inward conversion, a new heart, and a new man. To such an outlook, an established church tended to be only so much dead weight. The revival movement stressed individual conversion and piety, and the improvement of society by way of improved men and women. The way to community was not through government power but by changed people. Thus, the Great Awakening cut across the bounds of colonies and denomination to provide a common ground in evangelical religion to many inhabitants throughout the colonies.

One other development reduced the sharpness of the differences in religion from colony to colony and prepared the way for religious liberty. It was the abandonment of the belief in the use of political power to set up a religious heaven on earth. This belief had been strongest in New England, in the Penn colonies, and in Georgia. There were several landmarks on the way to the breakdown of the Puritan Commonwealth in Massachusetts: the Half-way Covenant in 1662, royal interference in the 1680s and 1690s, and the Salem Witchcraft Trials of 1692. The Half-way Covenant was an agreement among the clergy of Massachusetts and Connecticut that the children of church members could be admitted to membership though they lacked a personal experience of conversion. That tended to make the commonwealth more political than Puritan. Royal interference in the colony resulted in tolerance for Anglicans and reduced the power of the Puritans over the government. The witchcraft trials, in which people were convicted of practicing witchcraft and punished by the government aroused aversion to the use of political power to such dubious ends. The Penn experiment was never exclusive in the manner of the Puritan Commonwealth, but William Penn did cherish the notion of constructing a state along lines congenial to Quakers. Before the end of the colonial period, many Quakers came to believe that this was an error. The failure of the experiment in Georgia has already been related.

By the latter part of the 18th century, those colonists who had attempted it had been chastened by their experience with attempts at reconstructing society by the use of political power. They had been enlivened, too, by the idea of changing society by converting men rather than by the use of force. For some Americans, religion may have become less important than it was to their forebears. To many others, it was still of utmost importance, so important that it must not be dependent upon the expediencies of the exercise of political power. To virtually all Americans, it was their religious background through which they winnowed their experiences and in terms of which they built.

# Chapter 6
# The Mercantile Crunch

> *Although a Kingdom may be enriched by gifts received, or by purchases taken from some other Nations, yet these things are uncertain and of small consideration when they happen. The ordinary means therefore to encrease our wealth and treasure is by Forraign Trade, where wee must ever observe this rule: to sell more to strangers yearly than wee consume of theirs in value.*

> **—Thomas Mun,**
> ***England's Treasure by Forraign Trade, 1664.***

> *That wealth consists in money, or in gold and silver, is a popular notion....To grow rich is to get money; and wealth and money...are, in common language, considered as in every respect synonymous.*
>
> *A rich country, in the same manner as a rich man, is supposed to be a country abounding in money; and to heap up gold and silver in any country is supposed to be the readiest way to enrich it.*

> **—Adam Smith,**
> ***The Wealth of Nations, 1776.***

## Chronology

1634—England sets up Commission for Foreign Plantations.

1651—First Navigation Act.

1652-1654—First Dutch War.

1660—Second Navigation Act.

1663—Third Navigation Act.

1664-1667—Second Dutch War.

1689-1697—King William's War.

1699—Woolens Act.

1702-1713—War of the Spanish Succession.

1732—Hat Act.

1733—Molasses Act.

1740-1748—War of the Austrian Succession.

1750—Iron Act.

1754-1763—French and Indian War.

The colonists were not free to develop the economy along lines of their own choosing for their own benefit. True, an individual colonist who was a landholder had considerable leeway in producing what he would and selling it for his own benefit. But commerce with other colonies and with other nations was restricted in a variety of ways throughout the colonial period. Indeed, colonial governments restricted and attempted to promote or control economic development. But the main source of control over colonial development came from England. The colonies were part of an empire, and they were expected to benefit the mother country.

Historians sometimes claim that the British neglected their colonies. It has even been called "benign neglect," and some perceive great benefit to the colonies from the neglect. In fact, however, far too little attention has generally been paid to the extent to which British policy affected colonial development. It is true, of course, that the British government did not conceive a grand design of acquiring an empire and controlling it from the beginning. The empire took shape haphazardly, as first one company and then another was formed to settle in some location. Moreover, each company, group, or proprietor received an individual charter which differed in some respects from all the rest. Thus, the kind of control exercised from England often varied from colony to colony, in the early years of settlement at least. But the trend over the years was to bring all the colonies under a single system of control, especially in economic matters. Efforts along this line were begun as early as 1625, and a general system of economic control was in effect well before the beginning of the 18th century. It was not as thoroughly applied and enforced as it might have been in the 20th century, say, with our methods of transportation and communication, but given the difficulties of extending control at so great a distance, it was about as thorough as could have been expected.

The thrust of the economic control was to make the colonies dependent upon England, on the one hand, and to make them beneficial to England, on the other. The tendency of the controls was to place obstacles in the way of the colonies developing a close dependence upon one another or having an integrated American economy. Thus, while the colonies were becoming more alike and drawing closer together, the system imposed from England aimed at binding them more closely to England by dependence on her.

# *Mercantilism*

This system of political control over the colonial economy is known as mercantilism. The term apparently came into use after the fact; it was given currency by Adam Smith in 1776 when he referred to it as the "commercial or mercantile system." By that time it was under heavy attack, and Smith subjected it to a withering assault, even as he was describing, clarifying, and identifying it with greater precision as a system. Actually, mercantilism did not arise as an economic theory but as a bundle of political practices tied together by some widespread beliefs.

In essence, mercantilism is the practice of using the power of government to control the economy in the hope and expectation of increasing the wealth of *a* nation. It was not a device for increasing the wealth of nations generally but of a single nation. The method of mercantilism was monopolistic. That is, governments by gaining and granting monopolies to those whom they controlled hoped to increase the wealth under their control. A monopoly is an exclusive privilege to develop or trade in some good or product. Mercantilism is also sometimes described as economic nationalism.

The following beliefs and practices are mercantilistic:

1. **Bullionism**—This is the doctrine that a nation's wealth consists in its holdings of precious metals, i.e., gold and silver. To increase the wealth of a nation, then, it was necessary to increase its holdings of gold and silver. This was certainly a primary aim of mercantilist policies. Mercantilist practices began to become widespread in the 16th century. It is more than probable that several European countries developed mercantile practices in the attempt to separate the Spanish from their gold and silver. The Spanish got great quantities of precious metals from the New World and, aside from piracy, about the only way to get it was through trade.

2. **Favorable balance of trade**—This is a mercantilist phrase, or, at least, the term "favorable" is. Mercantilists consider a favorable balance of trade as one in which the country sells more in value of goods to other countries than it buys from them. That way, the difference would be made up in precious metals, thus increasing the wealth of the country with a favorable balance of trade.

3. **Promotion of manufacturing**—One way to obtain a favorable balance of trade was by manufacturing. That way, the value of goods shipped to other countries could be increased. Mercantilists often penalized the importing of finished products (with protective tariffs) and promoted the exporting of them. A variety of devices were employed to encourage manufacturing, i.e., the granting of monopolies, the payment of subsidies, and so on.

4. **Promotion of shipping**—The carrying trade was reckoned to be very important in getting a favorable balance of trade. The cost of shipping could be added to the price of goods in determining the balance of trade. Thus, mercantilist measures penalized foreign shippers and encouraged those of the home country.

5. **Planting of colonies**—There were several ways in which colonies might contribute to the wealth of a nation. First, there might be precious metals in the colonies. Second, colonies could serve as a source of raw materials for manufacturing or for agricultural products that could not be grown readily in the home country. Third, the colonies could serve as a market for the manufactured products of the home country. These last two might well augment the favorable balance of trade.

Above all, though, mercantilism was a system of government regulation, control, and direction of the economy. It was grounded not so much in economics—economics was in a rudimentary and fragmented stage until well into the 18th century—but in political thought and belief. Even the economic ideas that were in it derived largely from the spirit of absolutism of the age. Every age or era tends to have a prevailing outlook, a spirit of the times, so to speak, to which all its institutions, organizations, and social arrangements are made to conform, more or less. Even architecture, arts, and literature will be tinted and colored by this outlook. That is not to say that much from past ages may not endure, that all men will agree with the prevailing outlook, or that a great deal of freedom and differences may not exist within it. But if an age or era has a character, it arises from the prevailing outlook or spirit.

In any case, the dominant outlook of the 16th and 17th (and much of the 18th) centuries was absolutist. The prevailing view was that everything and everyone in a country must be brought under the power of the government, and usually of one person. The result of this was royal absolutism, theories of the Divine right of kings, and, in the 18th century, what was called Enlightened Despotism. These views and practices spread around Europe. The most thorough expression of this outlook in England was made by Thomas Hobbes (1588-1679) in a book called *The Leviathon*. Hobbes held that if people were left to their own devices, chaos would result. For, he said of people generally, "if their actions be directed according to their particular judgments, and particular appetites, they can expect thereby no defense, nor protection, neither against a common enemy, nor against the injuries of one another."

"The only way to erect such a common power," Hobbes continued, "is to confer all their power and strength upon one man, or one assembly of men, that may reduce all their wills, by plurality of voices, unto one will.'' The end result of this concentration of power was described by Hobbes this way:

> This is the generation of that great LEVIATHON, or rather, to speak more reverently, of that *mortal god*, to which we owe under the *immortal God*, our peace and defense. For by this authority, given him by every particular man in the commonwealth, he hath the use of so much power and strength conferred on him, that by terror thereof, he is enabled to perform the wills of them all, to peace at home, and mutual aid against their enemies abroad....
>
> And he that carrieth this...[power] is called *sovereign*, and said to have *sovereign power*; and every one besides, his subject.[29]

It was this outlook of the necessity to bring all men into subjection in order to forge a unity for the purposes of the nation that undergirded established churches, the centralization of power in the hands of monarchs, censorship, the granting of monopolies, and mercantilism in general. It was, to put it baldly, the fear of freedom, the fear of what harm men may do if they are free to pursue their own ends. Or, to turn it around, it was the belief that if men can only be controlled and directed in the common interest, great good may be accomplished. It has *not* been an uncommon belief in the course of history. Above all, though, it is the justification for the concentration of power and its exercise over people.

Not every country carried out mercantile control over the economy with the same fervor or thoroughness. The most rigorous control was attempted in France under Louis XIV (1643-1715). The agent for the imposition of mercantilism was Jean Baptiste Colbert. The connection between royal absolutism and mercantilism is best exposed, too, in the French development. He is called "the Sun King," declared that "I am the state," and few, if any, exceeded him in the exercise of personal power. Colbert applied mercantilism with such logical rigor that in France mercantilism was Colbertism. He attempted all those things that were supposed to bring wealth to a nation: bent the economy toward a favorable balance of trade, encouraged manufacturing, promoted shipping, tried to obtain colonies, subsidized business, "protected" France from imports, even encouraged early marriage to increase the number of French workmen, and forbade skilled workers to leave France by migration. He attempted to regulate the manufacture of goods in the minutest of detail in the hope that this would improve the quality of French goods and cause them to bring a higher price in foreign exchange. "The decrees for the period 1666-1730 filled four...volumes and totaled 2,200 pages. Three supplements, nearly as substantial, reinforced them.'' The regulations on cloth making consisted of 59 articles, and those on the dyeing of cloth, 160 articles. The tyrannical character of these regulations is revealed in the enforcement. ''Each had the force of law, behind each one was the King's authority....The intendant, the King's representative in each district, was responsible for the obedience of manufacturers and merchants. Therefore his agents made periodic...inspections. When they found cloth at any stage which fell below specification, their authority enabled them to slash it. This was the penalty for a first offense. Later transgressions brought fines or even imprisonment.''[30]

## British Mercantilism in the Colonies

British mercantilism was never as thoroughgoing as that of France. One major difference was that royal absolutism never reached the peak that it did in France. English kings were restrained by Parliament, and the rights of Englishmen set some bounds to government action. However, British control over colonial trade was imposed with considerable rigor. The English method of granting lands in the New World to private companies and proprietors not only resulted in considerable diversity from colony to colony but also enabled companies to trade with other countries. There were some early efforts to make colonies beneficial to the mother country. Charters usually specified that if precious metals were discovered in a colony a specified portion of those mined would have to be paid into the royal treasury. But since none of consequence were discovered, the provisions did not benefit England. There were some early efforts, too, of the British to gain control over particular products from the colonies. As soon as tobacco became an important crop in Virginia, the British claimed a monopoly of the trade in it. There were also some royal monopolies of trees for shipbuilding.

However, it was not until 1651 that the British attempted to impose a comprehensive system of control over colonial trade. This was the Navigation Act of 1651. This act contained many of the provisions that were common to all the navigation acts, but since it was passed by Parliament during the period when there was no king, it was believed to be invalid when monarchy was restored in 1660. Thus, the basic acts for the control of colonial trade were passed in 1660 and in 1663. The first of these acts required that all goods exported or imported from the colonies had to be carried in British built or British owned ships and that the ships must be manned predominantly by British nationals. All foreign merchants were excluded from the commerce of the English colonies, and certain enumerated articles, for example, could be exported from the colonies only to Britain or British possessions. Ships sailing from the colonies had to post bond that they would unload their cargo only in the British realm. The act of 1663, sometimes called the Staple Act, required that goods from the continent of Europe could only by imported to the colonies through England.

The purpose of these acts was to give a monopoly to England of trade with her colonies. Not, as one historian says,

> a monopoly to particular persons, but a national monopoly in which all English merchants should share. The Staple Act meant not only that English merchants would get the business of selling to the colonies but also that English manufacturers might dispose of their wares at an advantage in that the foreign goods which had to pass through England en route to the colonies might be taxed, thereby raising their prices and enabling English goods to undersell them. Similarly, the enumerated article principle assured that most of the colonial staples important to England would be exported by English merchants, who were also guaranteed employment of their vessels through the exclusion of foreign vessels from the English colonies.[31]

Later general acts of navigation had to do with providing stiffer penalties for violations and making enforcement more effective.

British particular legislation attempted to prevent specific kinds of manufacturing and trade from developing in the colonies. The Woolens Act of 1699 prohibited the export of wool or woolen goods from a colony either to other colonies or other countries. The Hat Act of 1732 prohibited the exporting of hats from the colony in which they were made, and limited the number of apprentices a hatmaker might have. Both these acts were efforts to prevent colonies from competing with English goods. The Molasses Act of 1733 placed high duties on molasses, sugar, and rum imported into the colonies from any source other than British colonies. This was an effort to force the mainland colonies to get these items only from the British West Indies and probably to reduce the shipping activities of New Englanders. The Iron Act of 1750 permitted pig iron to be exported from the colonies to England duty free, but prohibited the erection of new iron mills for making finished goods in the colonies.

Britain imposed other types of mercantile regulations as well. Once the British established regular mail ships to America, other vessels were prohibited to carry mail. Before 1663 neither gold bullion nor coins could be sent to the colonies. After 1663, coins could not be sent. The British tried to encourage production of wanted goods in the colonies by paying bounties. A bounty is a payment, usually by government, above the market price for producing something. Indigo, which was in demand in England for dyeing cloth, was supported by a bounty of 6 pence per pound produced. Also, naval stores were in great demand, and the British government paid 4 pounds per ton for pitch and tar, 3 pounds per ton for resin and turpentine, and 1 pound per ton for hemp.

In addition to such rules authorized by the British government, the government kept a watch over laws passed in the colonies and disallowed those contrary to British interests.

The purpose of all these regulations and restrictions was to make the colonies profitable to the mother country, of course. To that end, the colonists were encouraged to produce goods which could not be competitively produced in England, discouraged from competing with England, encouraged to send money to England and discouraged from receiving English coins, and prevented from developing markets in America for the export-import trade.

## *Colonial Mercantilism*

Although colonists often objected to and sometimes evaded English mercantilism imposed on them, their objection was more to its being imposed for the benefit of England than to the idea itself. Until well into the 18th century, most colonists were under the sway of the notion that government should impose an order on economic as well as other activities. Colonial governments were as much inclined as was the English government to impose their own mercantile regulations, when they could. As one economic history describes the situation: "it may be said that the Colonial governments were thoroughly imbued with the spirit of mercantilism and that government intervention in economic affairs was commonplace."[32]

One of the most common mercantile practices in the colonies was to give financial aid for the production of goods that were wanted. Colonies often sought to be self-sufficient, to avoid importing goods, as did countries under the sway of mercantilism generally. One way to get the desired production was to pay a bounty. Maryland, for example, offered a bounty of one pound of tobacco for every pound of hemp produced in the colony, and two pounds of tobacco for every pound of flax. This offering was first made in 1671, and several other colonies soon made similar bounty offers. South Carolina paid a bounty in addition to that offered by England for the growing of indigo. Prizes and premiums were sometimes offered by colonies, either for the production of superior products or new ones in a particular colony. For example, in 1693, Virginia began offering annual prizes for the three best pieces of linen produced there. In 1712 South Carolina undertook to pay 50 pounds to the first two persons establishing plants to produce potash.

Subsidies, monopolies, land grants, and other devices were also used to encourage new businesses. For example, Virginia provided a subsidy of 10,000 pounds of tobacco to an enterprise on condition that it produce 800 bushels of salt. "Massachusetts granted a twenty-one year monopoly to the Braintree ironmakers" to encourage them to produce iron.[33] New England governments appear to have gone in for land grants to get something produced more than other colonies. In 1735 Massachusetts granted 1,500 acres of land, plus a cash payment, to get an individual to produce large amounts of potash. Colonies sometimes encouraged particular kinds of activities by freeing those engaged in them from the payment of taxes. Another favorite device for encouraging production was to make it legal tender in payment for debts and taxes. Since commodities, such as tobacco, were often used in paying bills, this method of payment was not unusual or odd to colonists. (Money, for reasons to be explained below, was often reckoned to be in short supply.) An example of commodities being made legal tender to encourage their production occurred in 1682, when Virginia made flax, hemp, washed wool, tar, and lumber legal tender for debts.

Colonial governments also undertook to regulate and control trade. One object was to keep raw materials or unfinished goods in the colony so that they could be made more valuable in trade by finishing them. For example, several colonies prohibited the export of leather or hides. Another way to accomplish much the same result was to levy an export tax on wanted items. Georgia and North Carolina did this with leather and hides. Tariffs, taxes on imports, were common throughout the colonies. These were used both to raise revenue and to reduce the amount of goods from other countries being brought in. Reduction of foreign imports could have two purposes: (1) to protect domestic goods from competition, and (2) to cut down on the consumption of foreign goods. The latter purpose was probably dominant, for one writer says, "Even in Virginia, where indirect taxation was favoured..., import duties were designed almost as much for sumptuary purposes as for fiscal. This was true, for example, of the law of 1661, which imposed duties on rum and sugar."[34] The desire to cut down on consumption of foreign products was motivated by the effort to maintain a favorable balance of trade.

Colonies also regulated the quality of goods produced. Some of this regulation may have been to protect domestic consumers, but evidence points to a concern with the export trade, which made such regulation mercantilistic. As evidence of this, "In 1750, about seventy of the leading merchants in New York City petitioned the colonial assembly to provide inspection and regulation of flour milling because of 'the discredit our flour is in through all the islands of the West Indies.' As the result of this petition a comprehensive act was passed in 1751 'to prevent exportation of unmerchantable flour.'''[35] In addition to flour, ships, tobacco, meat, bread, and lumber were subjected to quality regulation in one or more colonies.

# The Impact of Mercantilism

Both politically and economically mercantilism is filled with contradictions. Politically, it turns international trade into competition between nations. Thus, it pits nation against nation, making trade more a political and military affair than an economic one. Economically, mercantilism is based upon a faulty premise. It holds that in trade one country benefits and the other loses. This is contrary to the most basic principle of trade that when exchanges are made both parties get something they want more than what they have. Thus, both sides benefit normally by freely entered into transactions. That being the case, the whole paraphernalia of mercantilism—favorable and unfavorable balances of trade, promotion of manufacturing, bounties, subsidies, tariffs, monetary restrictions, and so on—produces imbalances and rivalries that make trouble in many directions.

## 1. Mercantilism and War

The most dire result of mercantilism was war. The connection between the two was so close that some historians have concluded that nations adopted mercantilistic policies in order to prosecute their wars more effectively. One writer says that the needs "of constant warfare, especially its costs, had encouraged every power to develop and marshall its resources, attempting to become self-sufficient....This economic nationalism, generally described as *mercantilism*, is less a theory than a weapon—the use of economic means to serve political ends."[36] Undoubtedly, mercantilist methods have sometimes been utilized in making war, but there are good reasons for believing that they were more the cause of war than the consequence of it.

In the first place, the basic justifications that were offered for mercantilism were commercial, not military. It was supposed to increase the wealth of a nation. Second, mercantilist acts actually provoked wars sometimes, as we shall see. Third, there are clear reasons why mercantilism sets the stage for war. Mercantilism ranges government power behind the commercial activities of a nation, uses government power to support native tradesmen and shipping against those of other nations. On the other hand, other nations retaliate by adopting similar restrictions to protect their merchants. When trade is free of active government involvement, competition is peaceful. But mercantilism makes competition into a contest between governments. When governments contest for advantage actively and vigorously, they are headed toward their ultimate recourse—war. The quest for colonies, justified by mercantilism, aggravates the tendency toward war.

The conclusions from this analysis are borne out by the wars of the 17th and 18th centuries. War followed upon war with monotonous regularity as naval and colonial powers contested with one another for dominance and advantages. The wars between the British and the Dutch in the mid-17th century were clearly mercantile in character. The Netherlands had emerged as a major commercial power; they threatened to dominate in trade in areas where the British had a strong interest. The Navigation Act of 1651 was an effort to close off Dutch trade with British colonies. The Anglo-Dutch War of 1652-54 not only followed the act in time but was also set off by it. When the Navigation Acts of 1660 and 1663 indicated the permanence of these policies, plus clamping down on colonial trade with Europe, the Second Anglo-Dutch War followed. The desire for New York was a major factor in the British involvement in this war. When a third war broke out between them in 1672, the Dutch recaptured New York. But the colony was restored to England by the treaty of peace in 1674, and this ended the Dutch threat to England in the New World.

Unfortunately, it did not end the rivalry in North America nor the train of mercantilistic wars. France was emerging in the latter part of the 17th century as a major power in Europe. At first Louis courted the favor of English monarchs, but after 1688 and the Glorious Revolution the English and French were rivals in every European war that occurred until 1815. Indeed, it could be argued that France and England engaged in a new hundred years' war as they had at the close of the Middle Ages. Except their wars in the 18th century tended to become world wars. At any rate, as an English historian has said, "In every war colonies, commerce, and sea power were involved, and they generally constituted the chief interest of England in the war."[37]

England declared war on France in 1689. In English history it is known as King William's War, but when other European powers joined in it became known more generally as the War of the League of Augsburg. The war was fought mostly in Europe and involved mainly contests there. King William did, however, note in his declaration of war that French subjects had caused trouble for his colonies in America. Even so, no British forces undertook expeditions in America. However, the general war did provide an opening for New Englanders to try to put a stop to French Canadian incursions into territory they claimed. An expedition was sent by sea to Quebec, but it was defeated. The general war was ended in 1697, and there were no territorial changes in America.

The fate and prospects of English America were very much at stake in the wars of the 18th century, and the positions of European countries in America were greatly changed between 1700 and 1763. Political maps of North America in 1700 and 1763 indicate the scope of the changes and may suggest some of the issues. In 1700 the English held only a narrow strip of the eastern coast of America from New England to Georgia, with claims running back to the Appalachians generally. Most of the territory which is now Canada was then claimed by France along with the vast basin drained by the Mississippi. South and west of these were the extensive Spanish possessions. The English hold on the continent was still precarious, and the colonies were surrounded, except on the Atlantic Ocean side, by territory claimed by other European powers. This situation was dramatically altered by 1763 as a result of the wars.

The War of the Spanish Succession (1702-1713, known in England as Queen Anne's War) was fought over issues which were tied to the question of who would dominate America. Louis XIV was determined that his grandson should become king of Spain immediately and eventually succeed him to the throne of France. This would not only bring under one person two great European powers but would also link two massive empires in America. Thus, the war was fought not only to prevent an effective union of France and Spain but also to prevent a resurgent France from dominating American trade and colonies. The treaty ending the war contained provisions prohibiting the union of France and Spain. Britain also gained new territory in America: Newfoundland, Nova Scotia, and the Hudson Bay territory.

In 1739 war broke out between England and Spain, known in English history as the War of Jenkin's Ear. The trouble arose over English slave ships engaging in unauthorized trade with a Spanish colony. The war spread quickly, however, to spark a conflict mainly between Georgia and Spanish Florida. One of the reasons for founding Georgia had been to serve as a buffer between the Spanish and English colonies. General Oglethorpe led expeditions against the Spanish, and the Spanish retaliated against Georgia. No territory changed hands, however. In the midst of these developments, England got involved in war against France once again, the War of the Austrian Succession (1740-1748). The main conflict in America occurred along the border between French Canada and the northern English colonies. Although there were some English colonial victories, there were no territorial changes in the colonies.

The peace between wars was even briefer than usual this time. The conflict began, too, in the colonies, and was throughout as much or more an imperial than a European conflict. The war which got underway in 1754 in America is known as the French and Indian War (the

French and Indians on one side and the British and Americans on the other). War in Europe followed in 1756 and it is known as the Seven Years' War. The war in America initially involved disputed territory, mainly in what is now western Pennsylvania (Virginia claimed it at that time). Virginia land companies had been organized to promote settlement in the region. The French retaliated by building forts in the region and otherwise preparing to defend it. George Washington led the first attack, but his forces were repulsed. Combined British and American forces under General Edward Braddock made a large scale attack which was also turned back. Braddock died of wounds, and the new commander withdrew his forces to Philadelphia, leaving the frontiers exposed to the ensuing Indian attacks.

For the next two years the British and Americans lost ground in the conflict. George Washington did muster sufficient force to stave off the Indians in the Shenandoah Valley of Virginia. But in 1759 the tide of battle turned. General James Wolfe invaded Canada with a large force, attacking the French stronghold at Quebec. In the classic open field battle on the Plains of Abraham, outside the city of Quebec, Wolfe's army defeated the French under the command of Montcalm, though both commanders died before the battle was over. The next year Montreal fell and French resistance in America ended.

By the terms of the Peace of Paris of 1763 the British obtained all French territory east of the Mississippi and Canada, what had not already been obtained, as well. Spain ceded East and West Florida as well to the British. English America now included all of North America east of the Mississippi and the vast region of Canada. Technically, at least, the colonies had been freed from the threat of other European powers and the consequent need of British protection. Undoubtedly, this helped to set the stage for the American thrust to independence from England. But that might have been many years before it came had the British government not been in such a financial bind from fighting this long series of mercantilistic wars.

True, not all these wars, strung out over a period of more than 100 years, had been exclusively mercantilist in provocation or aims. Several of them—King William's War, War of the Spanish Succession, and War of the Austrian Succession—had supposedly been the result of dynastic quarrels, i.e., who was the rightful claimant to some throne. Although these claims were not entirely window dressing, they do not go very far to explain English involvement in them except possibly for King William's War. Moreover, commercial and colonial rivalries were involved in all the wars and in several of them they were major factors. The common thread running through all of them is mercantilism, though there were also dynastic, religious, and balance-of-powers questions in some of them.

The mercantile crunch of the British government is easy enough to describe. (It is correct to refer to the government as "British" at this time, for Great Britain was brought under one government in 1707 by the union of Scotland and England. Technically, the country is referred to as the United Kingdom.) These wars fought to defend and expand colonies and commerce had been very costly in lives, in materials, and in wealth. Moreover, the government had a large debt as a residue of the wars. The debt in 1755—just prior to the Seven Years' War—stood at about 75,000,000 pounds. By 1766 it had mounted to 133,000,000 pounds. The British had long been heavily taxed to finance these foreign ventures and new taxes were being added. The reaction to an added tax on domestic tax on cider is instructive. "The news of the passing of the cider act was the signal for 'tumults and riots' in the apple-growing counties of England, and many producers of cider threatened to cut down their orchards if the excise were collected."[38] It was this bind for new sources of revenue that prompted the government to tax the colonies, and this, in turn, set off the colonial resistance which resulted eventually in the break from Britain.

Nor is there any good reason to believe that the mercantile system, even in the absence of the costly wars and high taxes, would have worked to the benefit of the British people generally. One of the fallacies of mercantilism is that the wealth within a nation constitutes the wealth of a nation. Wealth in Britain was not distributed equally among the inhabitants; rather, it was possessed by individuals and families, according to their differing claims. Undoubtedly, some royal favorites, merchants, manufacturers, shippers, and tradesmen, prospered as a result of special favors, monopolies, and protections. Others, however, farmers generally, for example, may have benefited hardly at all. Indeed, when it is understood that mercantile policies restricted and taxed foreign goods and ships, it becomes clear that the populace often suffered from the higher prices which resulted. When the burden of taxes to pay for mercantile wars, subsidies, and so forth, was added to this —taxes levied generally—the British people were much more likely to be harmed than benefited by mercantilism.

## 2. Impact on Colonies

There is no way to be certain of the full impact of British mercantilism on the colonies. That colonies were disadvantaged by mercantilist policies can be shown, even that they suffered from debts and high prices induced by mercantilism, but how far mercantilism affected colonial development cannot be pinned down with any exactness. This is so primarily because we have no way of knowing how the colonies would have developed in the absence of mercantilism. Even so, there are logical connections between the way colonies did develop and English mercantile policies, and these had an impact on colonial development along certain lines, even when they may not have absolutely determined it.

British mercantilism affected the colonies from the conception to the planting to their growth and development. From the earliest settlements efforts were made to make them fit within the English commercial system. Companies and proprietors located in England applied pressure on the colonies to become fruitful in terms of the British commercial system, in short, to make them beneficial to people living in England. Once the government adopted general policies, these were even more pointed—aimed at benefiting the mother country.

There is good reason to believe that the Southern agricultural and plantation system was largely a product of British mercantile policies. The fastening of chattel slavery on the colonies generally and on the South in particular was aided and abetted by British policy. In the first place, the British conveniently overlooked the fact that there was no such status in British law. The laws establishing slavery could have been nullified in England because they were contrary to British law, but they were not. In the second place, the British engaged aggressively in the slave trade. Third, the British encouraged the growth of such crops as rice and indigo, which could only be produced in quantity by the use of slaves. Fourth, British policy opposed the emancipation of slaves, mainly because they were used as collateral for loans.

The tendency of British mercantile policies would have been to press all the colonies toward an exclusive reliance on agricultural and raw material production. It happened, however, that only the Southern colonies could produce many such products that did not compete with those of England, which is what was wanted. Thus the Southern colonies, encouraged by British merchants and colonial governments, produced tobacco, rice, indigo, naval stores, and some raw materials for export. The northern colonies, denied a market in Britain for their agricultural produce, sought other means of prospering: shipbuilding, the fur trade, shipping, selling food to the British West Indies, and serving as wholesalers and merchants for all the colonies. There might have been much more extensive manufacturing throughout the colonies, but British policies discouraged it when it was not prohibited.

Colonists were drawn into activities to increase their exports because of the desire for goods from Europe and especially England. Among goods generally imported into the colonies were such items as mill machinery, ship iron, canvas, shovels, axes, saws, chisels, grindstones, hammers, trowels, firearms, kettles, bowls, pans, dishes, saucers, buttons, thread, needles, lanterns, books, mirrors, woolens, lace, chests, chairs, and cradles. As an Englishman observed, "The American is apparelled from head to foot in our manufactures...he scarcely drinks,

sits, moves, labours or recreates himself, without contributing to the
...[enrichment] of the mother country."[39]

As one historian has said, "This import trade was the fundamental
fact around which revolved the economic development of the colonies.
From it sprang in large measure their value to England. The central feature of colonial trade was the exchange of American products for European wares; the central economic problem facing the colonies was that
of finding the means of paying for their imported supplies."[40] The
British mercantile system, if it worked at all as it was supposed to, made
it extremely difficult, if not impossible, for the colonists to solve the
economic problem.

The best way to see this is in terms of the balance of trade between
Britain and the American colonies and the colonial monetary difficulties. The colonies generally had an unfavorable balance of trade with
the mother country. That is, they bought more in value from Britain
than they sold in goods. On the face of it, looked at in the simplest
terms, this did not appear to be the case for all the colonies. In terms
simply of goods bought and sold, the Southern colonies had a favorable
balance of trade with Britain, and the Northern colonies had an unfavorable balance. For example, British customs records indicate that during the period 1698 to 1716 the Southern colonies bought an average
annually of goods from England valued at 154,200 pounds. By contrast, the colonies sold to England a yearly average of 245,900 pounds.
But these figures are quite misleading. They are estimated values in the
first place and the values were not market prices but prices estimated
before shipping. Colonial goods were subject to a variety of charges,
such as, freight charges, profits and commissions earned by English
merchants, insurance premiums, interest payments on debts, and the
costs of servants and slaves are not even figured in the balance of payments. Most of these uncalculated charges and costs were paid by the
colonists to the British or others. Moreover, British goods were apt to
be much higher in the colonies than when they were shipped from England. On the other hand, Northern colonies did not have as severe an
imbalance as export-import balances indicate. In any case, it is clear
from analysis of available evidence and the direction of indebtedness
that the colonies had an unfavorable balance of trade.

There was a deep contradiction in the British mercantile policies toward the colonies. The aim of these policies could only be achieved if
the British had a favorable balance of trade and the difference were
made up by payments in precious metals. Yet the American colonies
had no gold or silver mines or mints. They might have made up the difference by trade with other countries, and to a very limited extent they
did. But direct trade with northern European countries was prohibited and severely limited elsewhere. In fact, much of the difference in

the balance of trade was made up by loans of British merchants to the Americans. Many Americans, especially Southern planters, were in debt to British merchants from year to year. It was this fact which spurred them to buy more and more slaves and acquire more and more land in the vain hope of getting out of debt by producing larger crops. The system was rigged against them, for British merchants got much of the profit from the sale of tobacco and other staples; the government taxed them; the British monopolized most of their trade.

To make matters worse, there was the monetary problem. The colonies suffered from a shortage of coins throughout most of the colonial period, if not all of it. (Coins were virtually the only money that could be used in trade.) British policy prohibited the exporting of coins to the colonies, and such coins as the colonists obtained, such as Spanish coins, mostly wound up in being shipped to England to redress the imbalance of trade. It needs to be made clear, however, what is meant by a shortage of money. No particular amount of money is necessary to facilitate trade, and there was always some money in the colonies. But the colonies had a shortage in relation to the amount in circulation in England. The value of the money bears a close relation to the quantity of it in circulation in a land. The more there is in circulation the less its value. Since there was relatively more money in England and less in the colonies, the colonists paid higher prices for British goods than would have been the case if the money had been allowed to circulate freely. On the other hand, the British paid less for colonial goods, since coins could not be shipped to the colonies. Some colonies tried to correct this by placing a higher value on coins. The British government prohibited this practice. Some colonies also issued paper money, but the British government severely restricted that practice.

In short, the colonists were caught in the grip of a mercantile crunch. The British, too, were in a crunch because of mercantilism. When the British attempted to relieve theirs by taxing the colonies, they were following policies that could only worsen the situation for the colonists. Where would they get the specie to pay the taxes, when so many of them were already deeply in debt to the British?

But before pursuing this train of events, a major change in outlook in the colonies needs to be examined.

**Chapter 7**

# The Spread of Liberating Ideas

*The second great immunity of man is an original liberty in-*
*stamped upon his rational nature. He that intrudes upon this*
*liberty violates the law of nature.*
> —**John Wise,** *Vindication of the Government of*
> *New England Churches,* **1717.**

*A people really oppressed...by their sovereign, cannot well*
*be insensible when they are so oppressed....For a nation thus*
*abused to arise unanimously, and to resist their prince, even*
*to the dethroning him, is not criminal, but a reasonable way*
*of vindicating their liberties and just rights; it is making use*
*of the means...which God has put into their power, for*
*mutual and self-defense.*
> —**Jonathan Mayhew, "A Discourse Concerning Unlimited**
> **Submission,"** **1750.**

## Chronology

1636—Founding of Harvard College.

1647—Massachusetts requires towns to provide schools.

1687—Publication of Isaac Newton's *Principia Mathematica.*

1689—Publication of John Locke's *Two Treatises on Government.*

1693—Founding of College of William and Mary.

1701—Founding of Yale.

1704—Publication of first newspaper—Boston *News-Letter.*

1721—Publication of Cotton Mather's *Christian Philosopher.*

1732—Franklin begins publication of *Poor Richard's Almanac.*

1741—Publication of *The American Magazine.*

1745—Publication of Cadwallader Colden's *Principles of Action in Matter.*

1748—Publication of Montesquieu's *Spirit of the Laws.*

1766—Publication of Turgot's *Reflections on the Creation and Distribution of Wealth.*

1776—Publication of Adam Smith's *Wealth of Nations.*

The stage was set for the revolt against England, for American independence, and for establishing republican government well before these things happened. Many people had become Americans, not Europeans in exile, well before the final break. They had grown away from, even when they had not openly rejected, many European ways, customs, and practices. Legislation fashioned in a distant Parliament seemed foreign to these Americans. Many Americans had developed habits of manner and outlook little suited to subjection to any nobility. They could profess their loyalty to a British monarch the more easily because they never saw him and rarely enough any of his agents. Even British generals referred to them as Americans during the French and Indian War. The religious differences which had once separated the colonists so sharply from one another had been considerably narrowed by the middle of the 18th century. The immediate threat of foreign nations was greatly reduced at the end of the French and Indian War. The colonies were sufficiently populous, taken as a whole, for nationhood, even by European standards.

Even so, there are some counterpoints that need to be made. Though the colonies were growing away from England, their closest ties—economic, political, cultural, and military—were still with her. Although the name American was taking hold among them, there is little reason to doubt that even as late as 1770 most colonists still considered themselves loyal sons of Britain. (Indeed, even after the Declaration of Independence many clung tenaciously to that ancient loyalty.) Moreover, for those whose loyalty might be shifting, it would have been to their particular colonies rather than to any union. As late as 1754 not a single colony could be found to embrace the Albany Plan of Union. The clincher, however, is this: However much the colonists may have been prepared for the break when it came they did not make the break from England until they were repeatedly provoked.

The counterpoints are important, but it is even more important to be aware of the ways in which they were changing, changes that prepared them for independence when it came. None of these changes is so important, either, as the change in outlook. It is in terms of beliefs, ideas, angles from which things are viewed, perspective, assumptions, or philosophies that people are moved and act. Each person has his own particular views, shaped, enlivened, and colored by his own experience and temperament, of course. But in a given society, culture, or civilization there is usually a shared outlook that prevails. These outlooks shift and change, shed one emphasis and take on another, are molded into new configurations, and so on, from time to time over the years.

At any rate, there were major changes in the outlook of the colonists from the time of the early settlements to the break from England. Many of these changes occurred in England as well; some of them were broadly shared in European civilization, and they had great bearing on the belief in individual liberty, the rights of man, and the role of government. Since this shift in outlook had roots in ancient and modern thought, in Europe as well as America, it is well to examine how the colonists were connected to these, maintained the connections, that is, during the colonial period.

## *The Continuation of Classical Learning*

We might expect that when Europeans came to America they would have turned their backs on European experience, learning and culture. After all, they might have reasoned, America is different from Europe, and what was appropriate to Europe might have little bearing in America. There were different peoples here, different crops, and a natural setting in contrast to cultivated Europe. What could European schools, books, colleges, experience, habits of thought, and traditions have to do with the situation here? Above all, what relevance could ancient Greece and Rome have to the American setting and the problems of dealing with it? Indeed, would it not be more appropriate to imitate the Indians, go native, so to speak, and let the dead past of Europe bury its own dead?

There may have been settlers who thought in this fashion in the 17th century, but, if so, they left scant, if any, record of their reflections. The record we have shows a quite different attitude. Many of those who came to the New World showed much greater concern for preserving their literary heritage than they probably would have had they remained in Europe. The very danger that they, or their children, might not continue or be imbued with their heritage increased their resolve to take the steps necessary to keep it alive.

The Puritans of Massachusetts Bay had little more than settled in before they turned to the task of founding schools. As one of them said,

> After God had carried us safe to *New England*, and wee had builded our houses, provided necessaries for our livelihood, rear'd convenient places for Gods worship, and setled the Civill Government: One of the next things we longed for, and looked after was to advance *Learning* and perpetuate it to Posterity.[41]

The Boston Latin School was started in 1635. The age of the pupils in grammar schools, about 7 to 14 or 15, was about the same as for present day elementary and junior high schools, but there the similarity ends. Those who were admitted to these schools had already learned to read and write, and the grammar schools were devoted almost exclusively to the study of the Latin language and literature written in it. The older students also studied a little Greek. The Latin grammar school was preparation for college, and students usually went directly to college after graduation. But Bay colonists were not satisfied for long with merely having a grammar school. Provisions were made in 1636 for the starting of Harvard College. The early curriculum consisted of logic, rhetoric, Greek, Hebrew, ethics, and metaphysics. Since the study of languages was concerned mainly with the mastery of the great literature in them, the student who went through grammar school and college had learned, and presumably mastered, much of the classical heritage. In short, the earliest efforts at formal education in America were aimed at the continuation of Classical and Biblical studies.

Harvard was not, however, the first university conceived in English America. The Virginia House of Burgesses authorized one for that colony at its first session. Ten thousand acres of land were set aside for it in 1619, and money was subscribed for an Indian College and a Free School. Unfortunately, the school was completely destroyed in the Indian massacre of 1622. So it was 1693 before the College of William and Mary was founded in Virginia. Yale University was founded in 1701, the College of New Jersey (later Princeton) in 1746, Franklin's Academy (later the University of Pennsylvania) in 1751, King's College (later Columbia) in 1754, Rhode Island College (later Brown) in 1764, Queen's College (later Rutgers) in 1766, and Dartmouth College in 1769. While most of the colleges were founded in the late colonial period, the desire to continue the European educational traditions was in evidence from the earliest years.

It would be misleading, however, to convey the impression that the colonists conceived of education in the way it is thought of today. They rarely confused schooling with education. There were no state imposed educational systems. Massachusetts did enact a law in 1647 requiring towns with more than 50 householders to provide schools, and the Dutch had some tax supported schools in New York before the English took over the colony. But the Dutch schools were taken over and run by churches after the English conquest, and New England efforts to force towns to maintain schools did not come to much. Education was mainly a family responsibility in colonial America, and the extent was largely left up to the individual. There were no compulsory attendance laws enforced by governments. Most children got at least their early education in the home, where they might be taught to read, write, and figure, but almost certainly would be trained in housekeeping if they were girls, and in many of the tasks of making a living if they were boys. There were some schools in most of the colonies: church schools, schools provided by charity, as in Pennsylvania, or schools maintained by several families. A goodly number of towns had academies, or town schools, which were much less specialized than Latin grammar schools. But mostly, people did not receive more than the rudiments of an education in schools. Trades and professions were usually learned by serving an apprenticeship under someone who had mastered them. This was usually so whether it was carpentry, ironmaking, medicine, or the law.

The continuation of classical learning was much more the result of the efforts of individuals than of schools, though schooling played a role in it. The learning of the Ancients and the Moderns was kept alive, above all, by the books brought over from Europe or bought from there by colonists. Even the earliest settlers often made room in the little space on ships for at least some of their books. Although he died before he could use them, a Reverend John Goodborne, a minister of the Church of England, shipped to Virginia in 1635 works of the following authors: Homer, Aristotle, Thucydides, Socrates, Pindar, Seneca, Plautius, Terence, Ovid, Juvenal, Horace, Cicero, Plutarch, Virgil, Julius Caesar, and others. In short, he sent over much of the best of the thought of the Greeks and Romans. In the course of time, many individuals had put together rather large private libraries.

Among the largest of the private libraries were those of Cotton Mather of Boston and William Byrd II of Virginia. Mather, a clergyman and descendant of Puritan clergymen, had a library of close to 4,000 titles, and his writings are filled with classical allusions, which attests to the fact that he had consulted many of them. There were more than 3,600 volumes in Byrd's library when he died in 1744, more than 900 of which were from Roman and Greek classics. We know that he read many of them because of his account of his readings in his *Secret Diary*. As historian Louis B. Wright has said, "The humanistic tradition of the Renaissance, with its insistence upon the cultural discipline of Greek and Latin writers, exerted a strong influence upon the choice of books for American libraries." James Logan came to Pennsylvania as William Penn's secretary in 1699, and he put together a library of more than 3,000 volumes before his death in 1751. George Washington, who is not best known as a reader, had a personal library of more than 900 volumes.

Other than the classics, libraries were most apt to contain many books on religion and history. Although most would expect Puritans (and ministers generally) would have many books on religion, research has shown that collections throughout the colonies contained numerous religious works. "We forget," says Louis Wright, "that Puritans had no monopoly of pious reading; that works of divinity and books describing the means of attaining the good life were regarded as essential to every man who pretended to civilized culture....For example, Ralph Wormeley, secretary of the colony of the Virginia and a most unpuritan gentleman...collected during the last half of the seventeenth century 375 titles, of which more than 120 were books devoted to religion and morals....Few inventories fail to show a considerable proportion of religious books...."[43] History, too, held an important place in book collections. Among the books of the ancient Greeks and Romans many were histories; Sir Walter Raleigh's *History of the World* was a favorite among the moderns. Through the study of history, the colonists maintained their sense of continuity with past and their place in the scheme of things.

The reading in religion, in history, and in Classical and Biblical thought bore notable fruit in the debates that preceded the break from England, the great documents of the American Revolution, and in both state and national constitutions. As one historian has said, "During the discussions that preceded the Revolution and in the struggle itself, Aristotle and other classical authorities were cited on the superiority of the law of God and nature to that of human enactment. John Dickinson of Pennsylvania appealed to the *Antigone* as proof of the danger involved in violating the immutable law of nature. Demosthenes, Thucydides, Polybius, Plutarch, Cicero, and Tacitus were invoked to justify colonial resistance, and classical writers were quoted in support of the republican ideal."[44]

## *Colonial Literature*

Undoubtedly, the most effective literature produced in the American colonies was sermons. It was also the most common and widespread. Ministers were frequently the best educated men in their communities, had the most books at their disposal, and were apt to have done the most extensive reading. Sermons were not the brief speeches they have mostly become in our time, but were often lengthy expositions in which the minister displayed his ability to reason, his learning, and explained often difficult and involved doctrines. The sermon occupied the central place in most Protestant worship services, and, in some, it was virtually the whole of the undertaking. Not only that but sermons were commonly given at many public functions. Sermons generally were means of public instruction and inspiration.

There was little imaginative and virtually no frivolous literature produced in the colonies, and what little there was came in the middle of the 18th century. Most colonies did not have printing presses until well into the 18th century. None were permitted in some of the colonies;

Virginia did not get one until 1730. Massachusetts, by contrast, got its first one in 1639. For that, and other reasons, much more publishing occurred in New England than the colonies to the south. Some colonial writings were published in Europe; much that has since been published never appeared in print during the colonial period.

Aside from sermons, the most common literature written in America was histories, often combined with travel accounts and written as journals. The histories were usually of particular colonies or settlements, such as Plymouth, the Bay Colony, Virginia, and New York. No one attempted to write a history that combined all the English colonies; only from the point of view of England could such a history have had a unitary theme. There were two major purposes for writing such histories. One was to make a record of what occurred during the early years. The other was to build the reputation of the colony and lure settlers to America. To the latter end, there were often exuberant, sometimes exaggerated, accounts of the animal and plant life, of the fertility of the soil, and of the ease of life in America. An early description of Virginia (1613) told how the woods abounded with wild turkeys, greyhounds, pigeons, ducks, geese, and other birds. Of the inhabitants of the waters, he said: "Shads of a great bigness, and rockfish..., trouts, bass, flounders, and other dainty fish...." Thus, he admonished his English readers to "let not the fear of starving hereafter, or any other great want, dishearten your valiant minds from coming to a place of so great plenty."[45]

Among the more prominent of the histories were: William Bradford's *History of Plymouth Plantation*, John Winthrop's *Journals*, Robert Beverley's *The History and Present State of Virginia*, Thomas Hutchinson, *History of the Colony of Massachusetts Bay*, William Smith's *History of the Province of New York*, and William Stith's *The History of the First Discovery and Settlement of Virginia*. Probably the most charming of such works was William Byrd II's *Secret History of the Dividing Line*. It was written from his journals when he went on an expedition to the interior to determine the boundary between Virginia and North Carolina. It was not published until long after his death, but it was circulated among his friends. This work reveals another reason for writing history: to put down other colonies and build up your own. Here is the impression he gave of the laziness of North Carolinians:

> They make their wives rise out of their beds early in the morning, at the same time that they lie and snore, till the sun has risen one-third of his course, and dispersed all the unwholesome damps. Then, after stretching and yawning for half an hour, they light their pipes, and, under the protection of a cloud of smoke, venture out into the open air; though, if it happens to be ever so lit-

tle cold, they quickly return shivering into the chimney corner. When the weather is mild, they stand leaning with both their arms upon the cornfield fence, and gravely consider whether they had best go and take a small heat at the hoe: but generally find reasons to put it off till another time....To speak the truth, it is a thorough aversion to labor that makes people file off to North Carolina....[46]

Undoubtedly, it was such ideas that led the people of North Carolina eventually to describe their state as a valley of humility between two mountains of conceit (Virginia and South Carolina).

The nearest thing to imaginative literature in the colonial period produced in any quantity was poetry, and outside New England there was not much of that. The shift from the poetic to the prosaic outlook was already well underway. Still, writers did from time to time interrupt their prose with verse. And, it was very much the case, that when anyone would write of high, noble, and exalted matters, of the eternal and the glorious, of that which lies at the outer limits of the human reach, it had to be poetic, if not poetry. Indeed, it is generally believed that the first best seller printed in America was a poem. It was Michael Wigglesworth's *The Day of Doom*, a poetic rendering of the Second Coming and the Last Judgment. It was reprinted many times, but no copy has since been found from the first printing of nearly 2,000 copies. That has led to the conclusion that the copies were read so many times, and thumbed so often, that they fell apart.

Edward Taylor may well have been the best poet of the colonial period, though he was not well known in his own day. His poems were not published during his lifetime, and he left instructions in his will that they not be published. However, they were discovered in 1937, pub-

## Robert Beverley
## (Circa 1673-1722)

Beverley was a Virginia planter, whose plantation consisted of at least 37,000 acres. He was the son of a Virginian, educated in England, and married the sister of William Byrd II. Beverley took a fairly active interest in politics and served for a time in the Virginia House of Burgesses, representing Jamestown. His history of Virginia is one of the earliest, and is particularly valuable for the information he gives about the Indians.

lished in 1939, and critics have acclaimed him, if not a major poet, an important one. The power of his verse can be experienced in the following poem. The poem deals with the overflowing tide of God's love and of his own inability to return it in kind:

Oh, that my love might overflow my heart
To fire the same with love! For love I would,
But oh! my straitened breast! My lifeless spark!
My fireless flame! What chilly love and cold!
In measure small! In manner chilly! See!
Lord, blow the coal, Thy love enflame in me.[47]

Anne Bradstreet was another New England poet with a Puritan background. Her delicate and moving poems sometimes pressed toward the edges of Puritan orthodoxy; yet they always returned to the fold in the end.

## Anne Bradstreet
## (1612-1672)

She was born in England, the daughter of Thomas Bradley, and married Simon Bradstreet at the age of 16. They came to New England in 1630 in the midst of the Great Puritan Migration. She raised a large family, and, in what free time she could make, wrote poetry. In 1650, a collection of her poems was published as a book in London. Her poems show that a Puritan woman could laugh, love, speculate, and have great charm.

The three greatest literary figures of the colonial period, the only ones with any international following, were Cotton Mather (1663-1728), Jonathan Edwards (1703-1758), and Benjamin Franklin (1706-1790). Mather was certainly the most prolific writer in the New World, producing in all more than 450 books and pamphlets. There is no doubt, either, that he was a man of vast learning, not only in religion but also in history, science, and philosophy. His writings ranged from *Magnalia Christi Americana*, dripping with allusions to classical and modern writing, to the simple and straightforward *Essays to do Good*.

In addition to being an outstanding preacher of the Great Awakening, Jonathan Edwards was an original and learned philosopher. Edwards was a devout Christian, a strict Calvinist, and a man of large religious feeling. In his philosophical works, he reaffirmed the doctrines of Calvinism—that God saved whom he would through election, Original Sin, God's awesome majesty, and man's dependence on Him. Yet the will of man is free ultimately, and he is responsible for the wrongs that he does. In contrast to many of the later Puritans, he insisted on a personal experience of Salvation, that it was an inward experience, and he defended religious enthusiasm. His writings made him "better known abroad than at home"[48]; thus, he was one of the first American literary men to gain fame in Europe.

## Cotton Mather
## (1663-1728)

Mather was born and lived all his life in Boston. He was the son of a Congregational minister of note—Increase Mather—and was himself a minister in the same church. He held two degrees from Harvard, was a member of the Royal Society of London, and was awarded an honorary degree by the University of Aberdeen. He gained fame both for his belief in witches, has been blamed by some for the Salem Witchcraft Trials, and for his advocacy of inoculation for smallpox. In his voluminous writing, he displayed an acquaintance with much of the learning of his time.

The first two were New Englanders. So, too, was Benjamin Franklin —by birth and early upbringing. But he was certainly not a Puritan, and he did not remain a New Englander for long. He moved to Philadelphia and became an American, some say the first American. Franklin learned the trade of printer, became a publisher, and learned the art of writing. But he was a man of many attainments: an essayist, coiner of epigrams, economist, scientist, inventor, diplomat, statesman, and businessman. He exemplified better than any other person in America, except possibly Jefferson, the well-rounded man of parts, so much admired in the 18th century. All he lacked to be the complete gentleman was a large country estate, but there was hardly room for that in the midst of serving as postmaster for the colonies, founding an academy, and representing Pennsylvania in England. Several American universities conferred the doctor's degree on him, and his fame in Europe was almost as great as in America. Underlying much of his achievement and reputation was his way with the pen, his felicity of expression, and his literary acumen.

Both the continuation of classical learning and colonial literary activity provided the setting for the spread of liberating ideas. American

## Benjamin Franklin (1706-1790)

Franklin was born in Boston, went to school only briefly but became one of the most learned men of his time. He worked for a time as a boy in his father's tallow shop before going into printing with his brother. He went to live in Philadelphia at the age of 17, and it was there he made his fame and fortune. Among his many activities in an unusually varied and busy life, he was a publisher, scientist, inventor, statesman, and diplomat. He founded Philadelphia's first fire company, a debating society, a circulating library, and an academy, served in the Pennsylvania Assembly, as postmaster general for the colonies, in the Second Continental Congress, helped draft the Declaration of Independence, negotiated (with others) the treaty of peace ending the War for Independence, and served in the Constitutional Convention.

colonists were preserving their heritage, keeping up with developments in Europe, and beginning to make contributions to the literature and learning of their civilization as well. Nor were they simply dependent upon Europe and slavish imitators of what went on there; they were well prepared by the middle of the 18th century to make their own interpretations and to use ideas to their own purposes.

# *Science and Natural Law*

When Banjamin Franklin performed his famous kite experiments in 1752, he discovered that lightning *is* electricity. Since lightning is electricity, it is a natural phenomenon and can be expected to behave according to the laws governing electricity. Reasoning in this fashion, Franklin invented the lightning rod, a device to be placed on the tops of buildings to attract lightning and conduct the electricity harmlessly to the ground. In this cycle of activities, Franklin was doing what many thoughtful men among his contemporaries were engaged in. That is, he was finding out about the laws of nature and applying what he discovered to the affairs of men. This particular discovery belongs to a realm we refer to as science, but the natural laws men believed in and sought in the 18th century were much broader than that.

In 1788, the Reverend Charles Backus of Somers, Connecticut preached a sermon in which he had this to say:

> The present age is an enlightened one. Theories capable of being corrected and improved by experiment, have been greatly elucidated. Principles venerable for their antiquity, have been freely examined....The principles of civil liberty were never better understood. Conviction has generally obtained, that all mankind, of whatever color or descent, are by nature, equally entitled to freedom:—That voluntary associations are the only equitable origin of civil government; and that rulers as well as subjects are limited by the constitution. The rights of conscience, have been set in a clear and convincing light.[49]

Although his way of putting it may smack of pride, he does call attention to some fruitful connections that had been made between science, natural law, and natural rights.

The idea of natural law was not new to the 18th century, of course. Nor was it new to the 17th century. It had come to the fore in ancient Rome, had been greatly revived in the High Middle Ages, and philosophers and thinkers began to focus on it increasingly in the 17th century. The division of Christendom after the Protestant Reformation may have provided the impetus for this renewed interest. Men turned to natural law in the quest for a new basis of unity in a European civilization no longer held together by a common faith in the Roman Catholic Church. They succeeded in locating authority in the natural order, in the frame of the universe, so to speak, in natural law. The natural law framework provided a basis, too, for limiting and containing political power which had been dangerously concentrated and often exercised tyrannically in the wake of the Reformation. In short, natural law provided the basis for liberty.

Natural law has been used in several different ways. The ancient Romans used it primarily as a basis for a legal system with which to govern people in different countries which they conquered. Each people have their own customs, their own traditions, and their own laws, as a rule. If the Romans were to rule diverse peoples justly, they had to do so on the basis of something broader than these. What they hit upon were the natural laws, the laws that apply to people everywhere if they would have order and security, the natural laws of justice. But the natural law concept, then as later, had deeper roots than that, and it was certainly conceived much more broadly than a system of laws for governing diverse peoples in the 17th and 18th centuries. Natural laws came to refer to all those regularities that are to be found in the universe, in the

nature of man, the lower animals, plants, and which apply to the behavior of all natural objects.

The natural law philosophy in general got a great boost in the 17th
century from what we call scientific developments. These developments which are associated with the names of Francis Bacon, Rene
Descartes, Galileo, Johannes Kepler, Leibniz, Spinoza, and Isaac Newton were both spawned by the revived natural law philosophy and gave
new drive to it. These men not only believed that we live in an orderly
universe but also began to discover laws which they could state with
mathematical precision. This was so not only for such relatively simple
matters as the rate of acceleration of freely falling bodies but for the
relations between the stars and planets in the heavens. The poet, Alexander Pope, wrote of the most impressive of these discoveries in these
words of a couplet:

> Nature, and nature's laws lay hid in night,
> God said, let Newton be, and all was light.

Whether all was light or not, by the 18th century thinkers and research-
ers were questing for natural laws in many realms. They were looking
for the nature of things in politics, society, economics, religion, and
human relations in general.

There are several concepts basic to the natural law philosophy. One
of the most basic of these is the concept of a *state of nature*. Thinkers
of the 18th century often prefaced some statement with the phrase,
"Man, in a state of nature...." It is easy for us to misunderstand what
is meant by a state of nature, because we are accustomed to think his-
torically. Thus, we might ask, "When was man in a state of nature?"
Or, "Where are there people in a state of nature?" That is not the
meaning of the phrase, though some 18th century writers apparently
used it as if it were. The state of nature is an essential concept, not having to do with anything existing at some point of time. It refers to the
nature of a thing, as it is basically at any time, as it is minus everything
that is acquired from culture.

For example, to know the nature of man it is necessary to think of
him as he is naturally, to think of what distinguishes him from all other
creatures, to think of those natural attributes which belong to him as
man. As regards man, the state of nature refers to his essence. Thinking
in this fashion, the most general conclusion has been that man is a
rational animal, that he is capable of reason, and that this possibility
distinguishes him from all other creatures. But everything is understood
as having a nature within the natural law philosophy, is subject to the
laws of its nature, and is thereby a part of a natural order.

The state of nature concept is used, then, to discover the nature of things, the laws pertaining to them, and the consequences of actions. Everything has such a nature: governments as well as heavenly bodies, institutions as well as man; economies as well as natural objects. Nor was the state of nature a neutral concept during this period. The nature of a thing was believed to be implanted there by God, and it must be used in keeping with its nature or unwanted consequences would result.

Another basic concept of the natural law philosophy was the idea of the *social contract* or *compact*. The social contract consists of those conditions that are essential for men to live peaceably and effectively in society. It is not a written agreement, now do we knowingly enter into it at any particular time or place. Rather, it is that tacit agreement which is necessary, in the nature of things, to the fruitful existence of society. It is the consent we give, as willing participants in society, not to use violence to get our way, to respect the rights of others, to leave them to the enjoyment of the fruits of their labors, not to trespass on the property of others, to fulfill voluntary contracts, to keep our word, to honor our parents, to succor our children, to support the government, in a word, to follow the ways of peace. This social contract is the basis of social relations and, as men of the 18th century thought, underlies and undergirds constitutions.

Probably the most potent concept derived from natural law theory for the American colonists was the doctrine of *natural rights*. This is the doctrine that men have by nature, and as a gift of God, certain rights. They have been most commonly stated as the right to life, liberty, and property. John Adams described the position this way:

> All men are born free and *independent*, and have certain natural, essential, and unalienable rights, among which may be reckoned the right of enjoying and defending their lives and liberties; that of acquiring, possessing, and protecting property; in fine, that of seeking and obtaining their safety and happiness.[50]

Ample evidence will be provided further on that Americans generally believed in the natural law philosophy, used natural rights as the basis of the liberty they sought, and used these ideas to buttress their actions in the crucial years of the revolt from England and the establishment of governments. The relation of these ideas to the spread of liberty does need to be pinned down more precisely, however. It is possible to believe in natural law without believing that extensive individual liberty is desirable. Thomas Hobbes did. But the spectacle of a people establishing widespread liberty without being mightily impressed by a natural order is something that has rarely, if ever, been witnessed on this planet. The reason is this. If men generally do not believe strongly in a natural order they will tend to fall sway to the notion that their rulers must impose order into every nook and cranny of life. They will, therefore, have tyranny, not individual liberty. This is not at all because each person at any time might not like to do as he pleases but rather because he is afraid of the results if other people can do as they please. In any case, the belief in liberty in America flowered in a setting of belief in a natural order.

One other point does need noting here, however. Americans, who kept up with what was going on, were very much aware of scientific developments in Europe and made such contributions as they could to them. John Winthrop, Jr. (1606-1676) may have been the first American to be made a member of the Royal Society of London, and his most important scientific contributions were in astronomy. Thomas Brattle (1658-1713) made and reported on observations of Halley's Comet which were utilized by Sir Isaac Newton in his *Principia*. James Logan (1674-1751) set forth Newton's physics in the colonies, though Cotton Mather made a much more extensive explanation a little later in his book, *Christian Philosophy*. John Bartram (1699-1777) was most active in studying biology in America and making available information about it. The American Philosophical Society was organized in 1743, and it served both to spread scientific information and to gather it.

# The Classical Motif

Sometimes, the 18th century is referred to as the Age of the Enlightenment; at others, it is referred to as the Age of Reason, a continuation of an outlook that took shape in the 17th century. But in the arts—in painting, music, architecture, sculpture, landscaping, and so on—the dominant mode is best described as classical. In music particularly, the great productions of the period—symphonies, concertos, operas, and incidental music—are referred to as classical. (It is true that many people refer to the great music produced in Europe from the 17th through the 19th centuries, or thereabouts, as classical music, but that is a loose way of describing music which ranged from the Baroque through the Romantic and beyond by a single phrase.) The ancient antecedents of the artistic tone of the age were more Roman than Greek. That is important for American political development, for it was ancient Rome that had a constitution, was once a republic, and had a body called the senate—all revived in the United States. But that is not the aspect of classicism to be emphasized here.

Rather, it is the emphasis upon order, upon an underlying order, in the arts as elsewhere that was so characteristic of the era. It is similar to the natural law philosophy which was dominant in thought, for that had its springs in a natural order. The dominant motif in the arts was balance, symmetry, harmony, in a word, order. Every point must have a counterpoint, so to speak, every part on one side its counterpart on the other, every high matched with a low. The most characteristic architecture of the period is Georgian (named for the kings George of England, not the colony of Georgia). What Americans often refer to as colonial architecture—the Greek Revival buildings with their Ionic, Doric, and Corinthian crested columns—is not colonial at all. It is 19th century architecture. The contrast stands out clearly by comparing George Washington's Mt. Vernon, which is more or less Georgian, and Andrew Jackson's Hermitage, which is Greek Revival. A good place to see Georgian architecture in its variety and charm is in restored Colonial Williamsburg. The old Capitol building there is an excellent example of the balance and symmetry characteristic of classicism.

In music, the symphony best exemplified the classical motif. With never a discord, it proceeded harmoniously from its first movement, which was usually more varied, dashing, and contained contrasting elements, to the fourth movement, the finale, in which all was resolved. Mozart is credited with 41 symphonies, and Haydn with 104. Americans did not write symphonies—they could hardly have been performed in this country—, but they did dance to the minuet, which was often one of the lesser movements of the symphony. The minuet epitomized the grace, charm, balance, and stateliness of the classical mode. Even the sentences written in the 18th century often exemplified the balance and harmony of the classic. Here is one, for example, from Washington's Farewell Address: "This Government, the off-spring of our own choice, uninfluenced and unawed, adopted upon full investigation and mature deliberation, completely free in its principles, in the distribution of its powers, uniting security with energy, and containing within itself a provision for its own amendment, has a just claim to your confidence and support." Notice how word is balanced with word, phrase with phrase, suggesting finally the harmonious whole of the United States Constitution. It could well be that a part of the objection to adding a Bill of Rights to the Constitution was the fear that it would unbalance the document.

Above all, the classical motif was a calm assertion of mind over matter, of reason over the raw materials of nature. This is well demonstrated in the landscaping of the gardens of the 18th century. The hedges were neatly trimmed, usually ran in straight lines, formed squares and rectangles; earth and plants were civilized in them. Though men of the century spoke often of nature, they did not have in mind nature in the raw. Rather, they were thinking of the underlying order, the laws, the forms, and patterns which we discern by reasoning upon nature. The hand of man must cultivate, organize, and civilize all things before that order was revealed. The idea has been well illustrated in the description of a method of painting: "When a painter has made a draw-

### Gilbert Stuart
### (1755-1828)

Stuart was an American painter, born in Rhode Island and trained in England under Benjamin West. He quickly distinguished himself in England, and painted portraits of King George III and Louis XVI of France. Among American presidents whose portraits he painted were George Washington, John Adams, Thomas Jefferson, James Madison, and James Monroe. His portraits are famed for his ability to capture the character of his subjects.

ing from the living model, he should make another study of the same figure on a separate sheet....' Painters, in other words, should not imitate life but paint nature, 'not as it ordinarily appears, but as it ought to be in its greatest perfection.' Nature not as it is, but as it should be: eliminate the accidental, the incidental, the irregular, the distracting. Concentrate, select, simplify, purify.''[51] Undoubtedly, some such idea of painting informed Gilbert Stuart when he made his paintings of George Washington and other American presidents.

The most important point, however, is that the prevalence of the classical motif provided a sense of order and the role of man in enhancing it in his various structures.

## *John Locke and the Glorious Revolution*

It would not be accurate to think of liberating ideas as simply spreading from England to America. Certainly, liberating practices were hardly spread from England to America with a liberal hand. In fact, English rulers were almost as stingy with their liberties as with their gold coins so far as the colonists were concerned, keeping them at home rather than shipping them abroad. Many of the liberties which the colonists enjoyed were achieved by evading or ignoring British restrictions, resisting compulsions, and carving out their own claims to freedom.

Even so, England was a fount of expression of liberating ideas during the revolutionary struggles of the 17th century. Many of these ideas did take root in America, even when the practices were not extended to the colonies. Englishmen made daring appeals to natural law and natural rights, and it pleased Americans much to quote from them when they came to the point of separation from the mother country. Thus, it is important to review England's coming under the sway of liberating ideas.

The Glorious Revolution (1688-1689) was very much a watershed in English history. Theretofore, for the better part of 200 years, the English people had been subject to the rule of monarchs who were often stubborn, vain, arbitrary, and loath to admit that they ruled under constitutional limitations. Thereafter, monarchs were clearly limited, shared their powers with Parliament, and liberties were extended for the inhabitants for the following 200 years. The great age of expanding English liberties runs from 1689 to 1914, though they were not established all at once. It is called the *Glorious* Revolution for two reasons. First, it was a bloodless revolution. Second, it was a major step toward protecting the English from arbitrary government.

The Glorious Revolution came about in this way. James II came to the throne in 1685. He had trouble with Parliament for most of his brief reign. He was Roman Catholic, openly celebrated mass, and worked to remove the restrictions on Catholics. There were fears that he would unite with Louis XIV of France and advance the cause of Catholics against Protestants. When his wife gave birth to a son in 1688, there was no doubt that the child would be brought up a Catholic, and the probability was greatly increased that England was in for a long rule by Catholics. William of Orange (Netherlands) prepared to land an army in England, encouraged by some of the English. William was a grandson of Charles I and married to Mary, the daughter of James II. James fled England, and Parliament settled the crown on both William and Mary, as joint rulers. That was one side of the Glorious Revolution. The other side was the limiting of the powers of the king. These limitations were spelled out in the Bill of Rights (1689), which not only limited the monarch but also affirmed the independence and freedom of Parliament. Following this, England not only had a limited and constitutional monarchy but, even more important, limited government. The king was limited by Parliament and by an independent judiciary. The House of Lords was limited by the House of Commons, for only Commons could initiate appropriations. The House of Commons was limited by the voters, by the House of Lords, and by the monarch. Each of these had somewhat different sources of power: the House of Commons was elected; the members of the House of Lords either inherited their positions or were appointed by the king, and monarchy was hereditary. This system of separated and balanced powers served as the model for Montesquieu's *Spirit of the Laws* statement on the concept. No other concept was more highly valued when the Americans came to found their own governments.

The Glorious Revolution also provided the setting for John Locke's *Two Treatises on Government.* In it, he justified the revolution on the basis of natural law and natural rights. Locke was not the first to claim that men have natural rights or to justify them on the foundation of the natural law, but he did so in such a logical and persuasive fashion that the doctrine has often been credited to him. His thesis can be described this way. In a state of nature—that is, that condition in which men find themselves naturally if their institutions are stripped away—men have a "perfect freedom to order their actions, and dispose of their possessions and persons as they think fit, within the bounds of the law of nature, without asking leave or depending upon the will of any other man." In a state of nature, Locke held, man has a natural right to life, to liberty—that is, to the use of his own faculties (mind, senses, limbs, and so forth) for his own ends, and to property.

## John Locke
## (1632-1704)

Locke was an English philosopher, had a Puritan background, was much embroiled in controversy and sometimes in politics. His most famous philosophical work is an *Essay Concerning Human Understanding*. In this work, he argued that our knowledge is not innate but comes to us from sense impressions. He was an early (and late) advocate of religious toleration and wrote on such subjects as education, economics, political theory, and religion. Probably his greatest impact on the world was the natural rights doctrine.

Why, Locke asked, "If man in the state of nature be so free...will he give up this empire, and subject himself to the dominion and control of any other power?"[53] In short, why have government? Because, he said, of the "corruption and viciousness of degenerate men" they would not be able to defend their rights. "The great and chief end" for men to come under government "is the preservation of their property; to which in the state of nature there are many things wanting."[54] Thus, man enters into community with others for mutual protection and defense, yielding up so much of his powers as are necessary to defend him in the enjoyment of his natural rights. The "freedom of men under government is to have a standing rule to live by, common to every one of that society and made by the legislative power erected in it; a liberty to follow my own will in all things where that rule prescribes not; and not to be subject to the inconstant, uncertain, unknown, arbitrary will of another man; as freedom of nature is to be under no other restraint but the law of nature."[55]

Other Englishmen took up the cudgels for and sang the praises of liberty in the first half of the 18th century. Among these were two vigorous essayists, John Trenchard and Thomas Gordon. They advocated and supported freedom of speech and of press, security of property, religious toleration, and a broad range of rights for men. The foundation of their positions was in natural law and natural rights.

Regarding the origin of liberty, Trenchard said:

> All men are born free; Liberty is a Gift which they receive from God himself; nor can they alienate the same by Consent, though possibly they may forfeit it by Crimes.[56]

Gordon defined liberty as "the Power which every Man has over his own Actions, and his Right to enjoy the Fruit of his Labour, Art, and Industry, as far as by it he hurts not the Society, or any Members of it, by taking from any Member, or by hindering him from enjoying what he himself enjoys."[57] Regarding free speech and property, Gordon said, "Without Freedom of Thought, there can be no such thing as Wisdom; and no such Thing as publick Liberty, without Freedom of Speech. This sacred Privilege is so essential to free Government, that the Security of Property; and the Freedom of Speech, always go together...."[58] Of liberty in general, Gordon thought it an unqualified blessing:

> Can we ever over-rate it, or be too jealous of a Treasure which includes in it almost all Human Felicities? Or can we encourage too much those that contend for it and those that promote it? It is the Parent of Virtue, Pleasure, Plenty, and Security; and 'tis innocent as well as lovely. In all Contentions between Liberty and Power, the latter has almost constantly been the Aggressor. Liberty, if ever it produces any Evils, does also cure them....[59]

Thus, when the American colonists were ready to make their case against England and for their independence and liberty, they had a goodly heritage of arguments from English writers to which to appeal.

## Development of Self-Government

Both English and Americans believed that popular participation in government was essential to the protection of rights and the free exercise of their liberties. Locke argued that no man should have his property taken (be taxed) without his consent. The mode of the consent, of course, was to be represented in the body which initiated revenue measures. More broadly, however, for some, at least, of those who govern to have to stand for election provides a check against the arbitrary exercise of power. In any case, a goodly number of Americans gained considerable practical experience by serving in government before they gained independence. Thus, when they took on the full responsibility of governing, they had some preparation for it.

How they gained this political experience is best examined within the framework of colonial governments in the 18th century. There were three types of governments in the colonies: *royal* or crown, *proprietary*, and *charter*. A royal colony was one in which the colonial government was directly under the king. The governor was appointed by the monarch; in effect, he was an agent of the king. A proprietary colony was one in which the proprietor appointed the governor and many lesser officials in the colony. A charter colony was a colony operating on the basis of a charter granted by the monarch. These were the ones in which the colonists had the greatest control over their government. As a contemporary said, with some exaggeration: "The people in these Colonies chuse their Governors, Judges, Assemblymen, Counsellors, and all the rest of their Officers; and the King and Parliament has as much influence there as in the wilds of Tartary."[60] However, the trend over the years was for England to change charter and proprietary into royal colonies. By the middle of the 18th century there were only three proprietary and two charter colonies.

Despite the fact that the colonies had been planted and developed separately from one another, by the 18th century they had similar forms of government. That was not so surprising since they were modelled basically on the government of England. Each of them had a governor, whose powers over the colonies resembled those of the king over the United Kingdom. Governors usually had extensive powers: they were commanders-in-chief of the military force in their colonies, appointed members of councils, appointed judges, justices of the peace, sheriffs, and assorted other local officials. The governor was, of course, the chief executive in the colony; he could summon, adjourn, and dismiss legislatures, veto legislation, and pardon those convicted of crimes. He had large and extensive powers.

A colony ordinarily had one or more councils, but usually there was a single council which served in several capacities. It resembled most nearly a sort of combination of the House of Lords and the king's cabinet in the British government. The members of the council were usually men of wealth and standing in the colonies. In one of their capacities, the councils served as a governor's cabinet, advising him and executing his policies. In another capacity, they might serve as a court of appeals. They were the nearest thing to an upper house of the legislature that a colony ordinarily had. A goodly number of colonials got political experience by serving on councils.

However, most political experience at the level of the colony was gained by serving in legislative assemblies. This body was known by different names from colony to colony—i.e., House of Delegates, General Court, House of Burgesses, to name a few—but each of the colonies had one. It was the fount of popular government in the colonies, the only branch whose members were selected by the voters. In theory, it was subordinate to the governor in royal and proprietary colonies; he called it into session, could dismiss it, and could even dissolve one assembly and call for the election. He had an absolute veto over its actions. Thus, it might appear to be nothing more than an instrument of the government.

But, in this case, theory was one thing and practice another. The assemblies carried considerable weight because they could speak for the inhabitants. Nor were they above pointing this out to difficult governors. Moreover, colonists learned the subtleties and maneuvers by which power is counterbalanced in the hands of others and increased for themselves. The way they worked to do this is described by a scholar in the following passage:

> One is impressed with the rather prosaic manner in which the lower houses went about the task of extending their authority, with the infrequency of dramatic conflict. They gained much of their power in the course of routine business, quietly and simply extending and consolidating their authority by passing laws and establishing practices, the implications of which escaped both colonial executive and imperial authorities and were not always fully recognized even by the lower houses themselves. In this way they gradually extended their financial authority to include the powers to audit accounts of all public officers, to share in disbursing public funds, and eventually even to appoint officials concerned in collecting and handling revenues.[61]

Some of the devices by which they gained power are interesting and were quite valuable experience for colonists. One position from which they gained leverage over governors was that the salary of most of the governors was paid by their respective colonies. This meant that the legislature had to appropriate it. If they would appropriate it only on an annual basis, the governors found it expedient to call legislatures into session each year. Otherwise, they would have no salary. If they made the appropriation of his salary the last item of business before they were ready to adjourn, the governor could be, and was, effectively stripped of his power to dismiss the assembly before it was ready. "Not content with reducing the governor's legislative power, the assemblies... used their control over the purse to usurp many executive functions, insisting that certain conditions be met before appropriation bills were sanctioned. Thus the assemblies extended their sway over financial matters by stating in detail how money was to be spent, by appointing provincial treasurers..., by naming collectors of revenues..., and by setting up committees to supervise the spending of money appropriated."[62]

Colonists got political experience at two other levels than that of the colony. One level that did not involve many people directly but was nonetheless important was as agent for a colony to the government in England. An agent was sent from most colonies to England toward the end of the colonial period to explain to various governing bodies there the situation in particular colonies, the attitudes of the inhabitants, and the effects laws and other English actions might have. Sometimes both a governor and a legislature would send separate agents. They would have no official standing in the English government, but they were often valued for their services and would gain valuable diplomatic experience, for they were more diplomats than legislators. Benjamin Franklin undoubtedly got the most experience as agent, for he represented several colonies at one time. Through this experience, he was prepared for the yeoman work he would later perform in dealing with foreign governments for the United States.

The other level was local governments. In New England, town governments were run by town meetings of the voters. Thus, most males in New England gained some direct experience of participating in political decisions. In other parts of the country, county and parish governments handled most local affairs. Public service at the local level was often unpaid, voluntary, and many people served at one time or another. How local people gained control over and governed an English institution is well illustrated in the case of the Church of England in Virginia. In England, the bishop appointed local clergymen to their parish, and the members had little control over him. In Virginia, there was no bishop, so that the clergyman was chosen ordinarily by the vestry of the church. In theory, he would become somewhat independent of the local vestrymen when he was inducted into office and presented to the governor. However, in many parishes, the vestrymen never got around to presenting their pastor to the governor. They were able in that way to keep him on an annual contract basis and under their control. Some critics of the time complained that "they seldom present any Ministers, that they may by that Means keep them in more Subjection and Dependence."[63] That might well have been the case, but it is proper also to observe that the Virginians were tending to fit their churches into an American pattern of congregational control, and learning self-government in religion as elsewhere.

In any case, Americans had widespread experience in government, in legislatures, in towns, in counties, and in churches well before they assumed the full responsibility for government. They had picked up some attitudes, or drawn some conclusions, from their experience as well. Many had come to fear and distrust governments at great distance from them, particularly ones not under their control. They tended to prefer local governments to all others. Even so, the wisest among them believed in the necessity of restraints on all governments, though they valued less and less the British restraints. It is worth noting, too, that in the years just before the American revolt the number of lawyers in the colonies was increasing. Consequently, there were men not only trained in the law but experienced with the workings of government.

## *Adam Smith and a Free Economy*

One of the great liberating ideas which swept across the English speaking world in the course of the 18th century was that of freeing economic activities from the control of government. It was of a piece with the other liberating ideas of the century. It derived from the same natural law philosophy and natural rights doctrine. It proceeded from the belief in an underlying natural order, an order which worked best without government conpulsion and interference. In this, it was at one with the justifications for freedom of speech, freedom of the press, and freedom of religion. The movement for a free economy was most often conducted under the banner of free trade, but it was broader than that would suggest. It embraced the idea of the right of the individual to use his own faculties as he chose and the right to private property. But it got underway in opposition to mercantilism and all the assorted government grants, special privileges, and restrictions associated with it. Hence, free trade captured much of its appeal.

The first major extended statement of the position for a free economy in English was made in Adam Smith's *Wealth of Nations*, published in 1776. However, the movement toward freeing the economy was well underway before then. Following the Glorious Revolution many of the old restraints on trade were removed for the English, though not for the colonists. As an English economic historian has said, "In 1689 the Merchant Adventurers were shorn of most of their powers, and ordinary Englishmen became free to export cloth to all but certain reserved areas. In 1698 it was enacted that anyone might trade with Africa....And in the following year commerce with Russia and Newfoundland was declared open to all."[64] In 1701, a Chief Justice in England declared that all sorts of grants and charters in restraint of trade were generally void because of "the encouragement which the law gives to trade and honest industry." And, Parliament declared in 1702 that "Trade ought to be free and not restrained."[65] These were but straws in the wind, touching the right of Englishmen to trade in other lands, not the whole body of restraint and regulation, but they do indicate the beginning of a shift.

Even so, by this partial freeing of trade, economic practice outran economic theory. Such theory as there was—not much—tended to support mercantilism and government intervention in economy. But around the middle of the 18th century, this began to change dramatically. The French took the lead in setting forth the position for a free economy. Those who did so are known as Physiocrats, and they included such thinkers as Francois Quesnay and Turgot. Their conclusions have been described this way:

> They started with the axiom, common to all their contemporaries, of the rule of natural law in social phenomena. The circulation of money is as subject to natural forces as is the circulation of blood. The task of the economist is to ascertain the laws of nature; the task of the ruler is to apply them. In general, they thought, freedom in industry and trade would best allow healthy processes to operate and would suffice to promote general prosperity and happiness. The interests of society they thought best served by the self-interest of individuals, each working for his own profit. Hence, their maxim was expressed in the words "laissez faire, laissez passer"—let things alone, let them take their course.[66]

Although the thrust of their arguments was toward a free economy, they entangled it with a theory that has never received general acceptance, namely, that land is the root source of all wealth.

It was Adam Smith, however, who made the most devastating arguments against mercantilism and provided the most comprehensive case that had yet been made for a free economy. *The Wealth of Nations* is divided into two volumes. The first volume is an extensive setting forth of what we would now call the principles of economics. In it, he dealt with such subjects as the division of labor, prices, supply and demand, rent, capital, profit, and so on. Smith's plan was to expose to view a natural system of economy that occurs when people are free to produce and trade, a system moved by self-interest in the hope of gain, whose prices would be determined by supply and demand, in which the division of labor contributed to the general prosperity, and where the whole was held in balance by competition. Smith was to economics what Isaac Newton was to physics; his vision of an economy has the balance, symmetry, and harmony of Newton's conception of the universe. The second volume deals mainly with the fallacies of mercantilism, but also deals with such matters as taxation.

Smith's basic position was that if men are left free to pursue their own ends they will not only tend to increase their own wealth but that of others as well. That would be so, he held, because the individual could only prosper, justly, by producing so as to increase the supply of goods available generally. That would happen, however, only if government stopped trying to direct and control economic development. The crux of his position is found in the following statement:

> All systems either of preference or of restraint, therefore, being thus completely taken away, the obvious and simple system of natural liberty establishes itself of its own accord. Every man, as long as he does not violate the laws of justice, is left perfectly free to pursue his own interest his own way, and to bring both his industry and capital into competition with those of any other man, or order of men. The sovereign is completely discharged from a duty, in the attempting to perform which he must always be exposed to innumerable delusions, and for the proper performance of which no human wisdom or knowledge would ever be sufficient; the duty of superintending the industry of private people, and of directing it towards the employments most suitable to the interest of society. According to the system of natural liberty, the sovereign has only three duties to attend to...: first, the duty of protecting the society from the violence and invasion of other societies; secondly, the duty of protecting...every member of society from the injustice or oppression of every other member of it...; and, thirdly, the duty of erecting and maintaining certain public works and certain public institutions....[67]

Although Smith's work did not appear until the same year as the Declaration of Independence, some Americans were already leaning toward economic freedom, and in the years after its appearance they did much that was in accord with it.

# Chapter 8

# British Acts
# Become Oppressive

*What have these colonies to ask, while they continue free?
Or what have they to dread, but insidious attempts to subvert
their freedom?...*

*Let these truths be indelibly impressed on our minds—that
we cannot be HAPPY, without being FREE—that we cannot
be free, without being secure in our property—that we cannot
be secure in our property, if, without our consent, others
may, as by right, take it away—that taxes imposed on us by
parliament, do thus take it away—that duties laid for the sole
purpose of raising money are taxes—that attempts to lay such
duties should be instantly and firmly opposed—that this opposition can never be effectual, unless it is the united effort of
these provinces....*

*—John Dickinson,*
*Letters from a Farmer in Pennsylvania*

## Chronology

1760—George III crowned King of England.

1763—Proclamation prohibits settlement west of Appalachians.

1764—Sugar Act.

March 1765—Stamp Act.

October 1765—Stamp Act Congress.

1766—Repeal of the Stamp Act.

June 1767—Townshend Acts.

November 1767—Publication of Dickinson's *Letters from a Farmer in
Pennsylvania.*

March 1770—Boston Massacre.

April 1770—Repeal of most Townshend Duties.

1772—Formation of Committees of Correspondence.

May 1773—Tea Act.

December 1773—Boston Tea Party.

March-May 1774—Coercive Acts.

September 1774—First Continental Congress.

It may well be that the pivotal event which brought matters to such a head that the colonists began their overt resistance was the coming to the throne of the United Kingdom in 1760 of George III. He was the third of the Hanoverian monarchs of England, the grandson of George II (ruled 1727-1760), and the great grandson of George I (1714-1727). He was the first of this line of British rulers born in England, a fact he thought worth emphasizing. When George III came to the throne, he was in the first blush of manhood, and this promising young man might have been a welcome relief from the rule of his grandfather, who had no great regard for his own abilities. Indeed, the powers of the monarch had declined in the unsure hands of both George I and George II. During their reigns, it was commonly said that ministers were kings, and the Whigs had been the dominant political party so long that they had broken up into factions, each vying with the other to run the government.

It became clear rather quickly that George III intended to alter this state of affairs. He meant to bring the executive authority into his hands and to direct the course of Parliament as well. George III was a man of strong will—unbendably stubborn when he had made up his mind to do something—much courage, and, though young when he came to power, already aware of the means by which power could be concentrated.

One of his first acts as king was to remove William Pitt, the Elder, from leadership in the government. Pitt was a strong willed man himself, and George wanted men who would do his will. Beyond that, he moved to break up the dominance of the Whig party, claiming to dislike party rule. His method of controlling Parliament was not particularly subtle; he bought men to do what he wanted by giving them valuable offices. He visualized himself as a patriot king who would not only restore the glory of monarchy but also instill pride and greatness in the people over whom he ruled. He could sometimes control Parliament, but not so the great events, movements and developments that were underway in the world.

This new king's determination to rule as well as to reign affected the colonial situation in two ways particularly. First, the Whigs had much of their support from merchants and manufacturers who benefited from colonial trade. Hence, Whigs were much more inclined to accommodate the colonists than antagonize them by the use of force. For example, Pitt arranged to reimburse colonies for a portion of their expenses during the French and Indian War. When the Whig rule was broken up, men came to power who were much less attentive to the desires of the colonies. They were much more concerned with having the colonies pay their way within the empire than with increasing British trade.

Secondly, the new monarch consolidated his power by making many new appointments. Thus, he rewarded his friends in Parliament and increased the number of people who owed their positions to him. The need to have a large public service with which to operate was hardly the only reason for increasing the number of agents in the colonies and locating armies and navies there, but it served that purpose as well as others. Certainly, these actions did not endear him to the colonists.

There were events other than the coming to the throne of a new king which, though they did not produce the revolt directly, may have been the beginnings of resistance. One was a court case in Massachusetts in 1761. It involved British applications to a court in Massachusetts for writs of assistance. The British undertook to enforce the navigation acts more vigorously during the French and Indian War. To enable them to do that, writs of assistance had been issued in 1755, and new ones were being sought in 1761. A writ of assistance is similar to a search warrant, but it is much broader. Unlike a search warrant, it does not require that the place to be searched be named, that the goods sought be specified, nor have a fixed date of termination. It would enable officers to make searches for merchandise brought into the colonies illegally, without the usual restrictions.

James Otis, a lawyer in Massachusetts, opposed the issuing of new writs in a case before the court in the old townhouse in Boston. If Otis had stuck closely to the legal issue and argued that writs were unusual and rarely issued, this case would hardly have attracted attention. But he went much further than this: he declared that such writs were contrary to reason, and he denounced them as arbitrary and tyrannical by nature. According to one report of his speech, he said: "Every one with this writ may be a tyrant; if this commission be legal...Every man may reign secure in his petty tyranny, and spread terror and desolation around him." "I will," he proclaimed emotionally, "to my dying day oppose with all the powers and faculties God has given me, all such instruments of slavery on the one hand, and villainy on the other, as this writ of assistance is."[68]

James Otis lost this particular case, but as a result of his fiery defense he emerged as a leader in presenting and arguing the American cause. His local popularity was confirmed in the ensuing election when he became representative for Boston in the Massachusetts legislature. For the next several years he used his pen as well as his speaking abilities to set forth the rights of Americans and the limits of British rule.

## James Otis  ((1725-1783)

Otis was born in West Barnstable, Massachusetts, the son of a man by the same
name, who was a leading attorney and jurist in that colony. The younger James Otis
graduated from Harvard, learned law as an apprentice to an able lawyer, and began
the practice of law. He was a spark plug in defending American liberties from
British intrusions, opposed the issuing of writs of assistance, wrote several pamphlets
defending the colonial position, was a delegate to the Stamp Act Congress and
fought at the Battle of Bunker Hill. Illness prevented him from continuing his
leadership of the patriot cause during his later years. In the illustration above he is
shown protesting the Writs of Assistance before judges in the State House in
Boston.

Several events in 1763 both signaled a harder line from Britain and
the onset of a spirit of resistance in the colonies. One such event was the
establishment of a Proclamation line by the British in North America.
The British had acquired vast territory in Canada and west of the Appalachians to the Mississippi at the end of the French and Indian War.
The colonists were laying out land claims along the Ohio River and its
tributaries even before the war. Indeed, differences with the French
(and their Indian allies) about this territory had led to war. But the war
was hardly over before the Indians rebelled against the British, and
what followed is known as Pontiac's Rebellion (1763-64). This was going on when the British announced the Proclamation in these words:
"that no governor or Commander in chief of our other colonies or

plantations in America, do presume for the present, and until our further pleasure be known, to grant warrant of survey, or pass patents [titles] for any lands beyond the heads of sources of any of the rivers which fall into the Atlantic Ocean from the west or north west....''[69]

In short, it looked as if the British were going to deny the colonists any fruits of the victory. The colonists fought in the war, may even have instigated it, were now caught up in Pontiac's Rebellion, and were being denied the opoportunity of developing the region. The colonists did not resist openly; they simply began to push their frontiers westward. It might not be their right to settle in the region, but it would have taken more force than the British exerted to prevent it.

Another symptomatic event in 1763 was the one known as the "Parson's Cause." It was a court case arising out of the payment of the Anglican clergy in Virginia. A Virginia act of 1748 provided that each clergyman should have an annual income equal to the value of 16,000 pounds of tobacco. Bad crops in 1758 attended by rising tobacco prices prompted the Virginia legislature to pass an act which would allow all debts and taxes payable in tobacco to be paid at the rate of two pence per pound of tobacco, which was about one third what tobacco was bringing. The Privy Council in England disallowed the law, though in the meantime many had been paid at the lower rates. Some clergymen sued to make their parishes pay the full amount; among these was the famous suit brought by the Reverend James Maury. The court declared that the Virginia law had been invalid and sent the case to trial before a jury to determine the amount of damages due to Mr. Maury.

Patrick Henry played a major role at the trial, in opposition to the Maury suit. Henry was not well known until this trial. During early manhood he had bounced from one undertaking to another until he studied law briefly. Whatever his legal qualifications he was an outstanding orator, and because of his daring and outspoken defense his fame spread around Virginia. According to Mr. Maury, who was, of course, a biased witness, Henry "harrangued the jury for near an hour" toward the close of the case known as the "Parson's Cause." He argued that the Virginia act of 1758 met all the qualifications of good law, and "that a King, by disallowing Acts of this salutary nature, from being the father of his people degenerated into a Tyrant and forfeits all right to his subjects' obedience."[70] Moreover, he declared that it was the duty of the clergy of an established church to support law, and not to be going into the courts to challenge it. The jury upheld Mr. Maury's claim, as it was told by the court it must, and awarded him one penny for his losses. Technically, British rule had been vindicated, but it was clear that Henry had, in fact, won the case. His remarks about the king's becoming a tyrant were greeted with murmurs of "treason," but neither judge nor jury censured him.

## Patrick Henry
## (1736-1799)

Henry was one of the most daring and out-spoken opponents of British policies from the first hint of resistance to the Declaration of Independence. He was born in Hanover County, Virginia, operated a store, farmed, and eventually studied law briefly before going into practice. He served in the Virginia House of Burgesses, was a leader in opposing the Stamp Act, was among the most fiery advocates of independence, and served in the Second Continental Congress. He helped to draft the Virginia constitution and served as governor of the new state. In the Virginia Convention for ratification of the United States Constitution, Henry led the last ditch fight for a bill of rights.

None of this should be interpreted to mean that the colonists were ready to break from England in 1763. On the contrary, to all outward appearances the old ties were still in place. Colonists continued well into 1776 to affirm their loyalty to the British monarch. Undoubtedly, the general developments which set the stage for American independence had taken place by 1763. Americans had developed practices in religion which distinguished them from their British forebears. Feudal relics and mercantile and religious restrictions were not much in keeping with the emerging American temper. Colonists had much experience in politics which prepared them for governing themselves. The natural law philosophy was familiar to many Americans, and it would serve as a basis for breaking from England and erecting new governments. Population had grown to a point where the colonists could contemplate independence. But it was changes in British policy which provoked colonial resistance, led colonists to examine with ever greater care the character of British rule, and drove them to the breaking point.

## *The First Crisis—1764-1766*

In April 1763, George Grenville became Chancellor of the Exchequer and formed a new government in Britain. Grenville was responsible for two major courses of change toward the colonies. One was the tightening of administration and enforcement of the laws. The other was the passage of laws which were aimed at raising revenue from the colonies.

An apparently casual action by Parliament in 1763 set the stage for much that followed. Funds were voted for maintaining a standing army in America. This was handled without much ado, since there was already an army in America. Grenville had a direct hand in the subsequent stationing of naval vessels in America. He was First Lord of the Admiralty and got a law passed giving naval officers the power to act as customs officials. By the fall of 1763 naval vessels were patrolling the waters from Newfoundland to the West Indies seeking ships carrying illegal cargo. A profound change was occurring between Britain and her colonies, and the decision to have military power available was the signal of a determination to crack down on the colonies.

That Grenville meant business was clear from the new orders he gave concerning customs officials. Appointments to major customs ports in America had long been sources of income to their holders who put little effort into the jobs. Quite often, they drew their pay while continuing to reside in Britain. Grenville decreed that henceforth they must live in America. Many resigned rather than go to the colonies and new officers were appointed in their places.

In 1764 Grenville pushed through a new legislative program designed to get revenue from the colonies. The key piece of legislation is usually called the Sugar Act, though it dealt with much more than sugar. The act lowered the tariffs on molasses coming into the colonies, prohibited the importation of rum, added items to the enumerated lists, and provided strenuous regulations on shipping. The greatest departure from precedent in it was that it was aimed to raise tax money for the British government. The preamble of the act reads, in part: "Whereas it is expedient that new provisions and regulations should be established for improving the revenue of this kingdom...: and whereas it is just and necessary that a revenue be raised in your Majesty's said dominions in America, for defraying the expenses of defending, protecting, and securing the same; we...have resolved to give and grant unto your Majesty the several rates and duties herein after mentioned."[71]

At the outset the regulations on shipping may have been more burdensome than the revenue measures. Captains of vessels in the trade with the West Indies had to have affidavits, certificates, complete lists of goods, and had to post bond guaranteeing they were in compliance with the law. Moreover, if their ships were seized by British authorities the burden of proof remained on them before they could reclaim their ships. The act declared that "if any ship or goods shall be seized for any cause of forfeiture, and any dispute shall arise whether the customs and duties for such goods have been paid, or the same have been lawfully imported or exported, or concerning the growth, product, or manufacture, of such goods..., the proof thereof shall lie upon the owner or claimer."[72] In addition the act mandated the decisions juries were to reach for particular acts, thus taking most of their discretionary powers from them. In short, customs officials were given virtually a free hand and the colonists were left with little protection against them.

The colonists had hardly had time to assess the impact of these acts before Parliament passed yet another revenue measure. The Stamp Act was passed in March of 1765. It required that after November 1, 1765, stamps be affixed to all legal papers, commercial papers, liquor licenses, land documents, indentures, cards, dice, pamphlets, newspapers, advertisements, almanacs, academic degrees and appointments to office. The money collected from the sale of these revenue (not postage) stamps was to go to the British treasury to be used for expenses incurred in America. This act was the most clear-cut departure from tradition yet made by the British government, for it placed a direct tax on the Americans, something that had not been done before. More, it fell upon the most vocal people in America: lawyers and publishers.

The Stamp Act was followed in short order by an indirect taxing measure, an act known as the Quartering Act, passed in May of 1765. It provided for the quartering of troops in alehouses, inns, unoccupied dwellings, and in buildings belonging to colonial governments. That much might have occasioned no great difficulty, but the act also provided that "all such officers and soldiers...be furnished and supplied...with fire, candles, vinegar, and salt, bedding, utensils...without paying anything for the same."[73] In short, the colonies were indirectly taxed for the maintaining of British troops in quarters; they might levy such taxes themselves, but they would do so under compulsion.

However, the fat was in the fire well before news of the Quartering Act had reached America. Even before the Stamp Act had been passed there was opposition to the Grenville acts. Boston appointed a committee to correspond with other colonies about the disadvantages of the Sugar Act. The New York legislature denied the rightfulness of such duties and questioned that taxes should be imposed on them by other bodies.

But it was resistance to the Stamp Act that drew the colonies together in a show of unity of opposition. Opposition was shaping up before the tax had been passed. Opponents in Parliament challenged the legality of the tax. When Charles Townshend asked: "Will these Americans, children planted by our care, nourished up by our indulgence..., will they grudge to contribute their mite...?" he was answered in resounding terms in a speech by Sir Isaac Barre:

> They planted by your care? No! Your oppressions planted 'em in America. They fled from your oppression....
>
> They nourished by your indulgence? They grew up by your neglect of 'em. As soon as you began to care about 'em, that care was exercised in sending persons to rule over 'em....
>
> They protected by your arms? They have nobly taken up arms in your defence....[74]

This was the famous "Sons of Liberty" speech, for Barre used the phrase, and Americans took it up to apply to organizations of that name. Before the Stamp Act was passed, several colonial legislatures went on record as opposing it. All this was to no avail, the die had been cast in 1764, and Parliament proceeded to the enactment of a direct tax.

Not only was Parliament mistaken as to the probable reception of the Stamp Act in America, but even colonial agents representing the colonies in England had misjudged American sentiment and determination. Several colonial representatives accepted commissions as stamp agents, actions which they were to regret. Even the usually wise Benjamin Franklin caused friends to be appointed stamp agents and expressed himself of the opinion that the proper course would be to abide by the law.

Whether it would have been wise to have done so or not, obedience was not the course followed in America. On the contrary, Americans moved from opposition to resistance to outright defiance. Colonial legislatures adopted resolutions against the tax. Virginia led the way under the prodding of Patrick Henry. He charged that the Stamp Act was an act of tyranny, and was reported as saying, "Tarquin and Caesar had each his Brutus, Charles the First his Cromwell, and George the Third..." The Speaker of the House interrupted to declare that he had spoken "Treason!" With only a brief pause, Henry continued: "...may profit by their example! If *this* be treason, make the most of it."[75] Not all of Henry's resolutions were adopted by the House of Burgesses (though they were all published in newspapers), but of those that were, the following gives the crux of the argument:

> *Resolved.* That the taxation of the people by themselves or by persons chosen by themselves to represent them, who can only know what taxes the people are able to bear, are the easiest method of raising them, and must themselves be affected by every tax laid on the people, is the only security against a burthensome taxation, and the distinguishing characteristick of British freedom, without which the ancient constitution cannot exist.[76]

Massachusetts took the lead in calling for common action among the colonies. The legislative assembly sent out a call for a congress of all the colonies. As a result, a Stamp Act Congress met in New York in October of 1765. Six colonial legislatures appointed delegates to it, and three others had representatives not so formally chosen. The delegates in Congress assembled affirmed their allegience to the king and their willing subordination to Parliament when it acted properly. But they resolved that there were limits to this authority, some of which they spelled out:

That it is inseparably essential to the freedom of a people, and the undoubted right of Englishmen, that no taxes be imposed on them but with their own consent, given personally or by their representatives....

That the only representatives of the people of these colonies are persons chosen therein by themselves, and that no taxes ever have been or can be constitutionally imposed on them, but by their respective legislatures.[77]

But the colonists were not content with merely adopting resolutions and making appeals to Britain. They took direct action to see to it that the Stamp Act was not enforced. The Committees of Correspondence laid the groundwork for the direct action and much of it was done by the Sons of Liberty. (These were private associations, it should be noted, not organs of government.) The first effort was to secure the resignation of stamp agents, who were charged with the duty of selling the stamps. In some colonies, stamp agents resigned when they recognized the unpopularity of their undertaking. In others they held out for awhile, and were subject to threats, abuse and humiliation. The case of Jared Ingersoll of Connecticut, who had accepted an appointment as stamp agent while in England as colonial representative, shows the lengths to which crowds went sometimes to secure the resignation of obstinate agents. "They caught Ingersoll at Wethersfield and silently and pointedly led him under a large tree. They parlayed for hours..., with Ingersoll squirming, arguing and refusing to resign. The crowds...grew so large and threatening that finally Ingersoll read his resignation to the mob and yielded to the demand that he throw his hat in the air and cheer for 'Liberty and Property.' "[78] Others who held out received similar, or worse, treatment.

So successful was this direct effort that on the day that the Stamp Act was to go into effect there were no stamps available in the colonies. The question now was whether business would go on as usual in defiance of the law. If the law were observed, ships would not sail, courts would not hold sessions, newpapers would not be published, and much of life would come to a standstill. In fact, many newspapers continued to be published and sold; ships sailed, and some courts carried on business as usual, their documents unstamped. By and large, the colonies operated in defiance of the law.

When Parliament convened in December 1765, it was confronted by a crisis in America of its own making. However, the king's opening address to Parliament only acknowledged that "matters of importance have lately occurred in some of my colonies in America...."[79] Even so, Parliament had to take some kind of action. Either it would have to take stern measures to accomplish compliance or back down.

Grenville's ministry had already fallen, and a new government was organized under the leadership of Rockingham. With the matchless orator William Pitt, Earl of Chatham, taking the lead in the debate for repeal, the House voted 275 to 167 in favor of repeal. Shortly thereafter the bill became a law. However, Parliament refused to yield on the principle of its powers of taxation, for it insisted on passing a Declaratory Act, which went into effect on the same day that the Stamp Act was repealed. It declared "that the King's majesty, by and with the advice and consent of the lords spiritual and temporal, and commons of *Great Britain*, in parliament assembled, had, hath, and of right ought to have, full power and authority to make laws and statutes of sufficient force and validity to bind the colonies...in all cases whatsoever."[80]

The issue was still joined, if Parliament be taken at its face-saving word, but the first crisis had ended. Actually, most of the Grenville measures were still in effect—the stationing of the military in America, the Sugar Act, the Quartering Act and the restraints on colonial juries. The Proclamation Line was not altered until 1768. Even as the Stamp Act repeal had barely been achieved, the New York Sons of Liberty advised that it would be in order to go ahead and press for removal of all the restrictions on trade. But the colonists had made the Stamp Act *the* issue, and, with its repeal, resistance eased. The case against direct internal taxes imposed by Parliament was clear and on solid ground, many believed, but the case against taxation, *per se*, had yet to be developed.

The issue that had been joined might better be called a budding issue. It was a long way from maturity in 1765. The question was the extent of the authority of the British Parliament over the colonies. The colonists were of the view that the authority was limited. One of the limits, the legislature of Connecticut said in 1765, is this:

> That, in the opinion of this House, an act for raising money by duties or taxes differs from other acts of legislation, in that it is always considered as a free gift of the people made by their legal and elected representatives; and that we cannot conceive that the people of Great Britain, or their representatives, have right to dispose of our property.[81]

On the other hand, Richard Bland of Virginia, writing in 1766, doubted that the extent of parliamentary authority had ever been determined. "It is in vain to search into the civil constitution of *England*," he said, "for directions in fixing the proper connection between the colonies and the mother-kingdom.... The planting of colonies from *Britain* is but of recent date, and nothing relative to such plantation can be collected from the ancient laws of the kingdom...." In consequence, he argued, "As then we can receive no light from the laws of the kingdom, or from ancient history to direct us in our enquiry, we must have recourse to the law of nature, and those rights of mankind which flow from it." But to appeal to the natural law at this stage would be premature. Parliament, of course, had taken the position that its acts were binding in all cases whatsoever. There the matter stood in 1766.

One point needs to be born in mind in all the discussion of colonial opposition to British action. The colonists were quite limited in the legal means available to them. Generally, they did not fully control the colonial governments. Except in the charter colonies of Connecticut and Rhode Island, they did not choose their governors. Thus, the executive power in the colony was denied to the colonists. As a rule, governors selected the members of their council. The legislative assembly was popularly elected, but the governor had great powers of restraint over it. Nor was there any established means for intercolonial action. None had ever been set up, and the British were hardly inclined to favor any such bodies at this time. At best, only extra-legal means were available for concerted action across the lines of colonies, such means as the temporary Stamp Act Congress. Thus, the colonists had to resist cautiously, else they would become outlaws.

## *The Townshend Acts*

For a time after the repeal of the Stamp Act, it looked as if the British would stay their hand with the colonies. William Pitt formed a cabinet and he had taken a generous view toward the colonies during the debate over stamps. Indeed, Pitt was far and away the most popular Englishman in America, though truth to tell he had little competition. But Pitt was made Earl of Chatham, moved into the House of Lords, and was in poor health, in any case. In 1767 the leadership in Commons passed to Charles Townshend, Chancellor of the Exchequer. The government still suffered from its financial difficulties, especially the debts left over from mercantile wars. Townshend believed that the colonies still offered opportunities for raising money. Thus, he passed through Parliament a series of acts in 1767.

The act which drew the most attention was the one levying import duties on glass, lead, painter's colors, paper and tea. During the debates over the stamp tax the distinction between internal and external was talked about considerably. For that reason, the British drew the conclusion that Americans accepted external taxes, but not internal ones. Operating from this premise, Townshend argued that Americans should accept these new duties, since they were levied on imports and could be considered external taxes. The act indicated that it was for the purpose of raising revenue, that such monies as were raised would go first to defray costs of governing America, that what was left would go into the British treasury, and that the duties must be paid in silver. It also authorized the use of writs of assistance to be used in searching for goods on which duties had not been paid and empowered "his Majesty's customs to enter and go into any house, warehouse, shop, cellar, or other place, in the *British* colonies or plantations in America, to search for and seize prohibited or uncustomed goods" with writs which courts in America were directed to issue.

Another act, passed at the same time, was the American Board of Customs Act. This established a board of customs for America, to be composed of five commissioners, and to be located at Boston. A little later in the year, an act was passed suspending the New York legislature for not providing troop supplies. In a similar vein, an act in September 1767 curtailed the power of colonial legislatures generally. The tenor of these acts was not only to facilitate the raising of revenue but also to reduce colonial control over their own affairs. Along these same lines, an act passed in July of 1768 extended and spelled out the jurisdictions of vice-admiralty courts in the colonies and increased the number of courts in America from one to four. These were, in effect, military (naval) courts being given jurisdiction over civilians.

The colonists did not react with the same swiftness they had to the stamp taxes. The stamp tax was, after all, different from any that had been levied on colonists from Britain before. By contrast, the Townshend duties were similar to some already in effect and were at least distantly related to regulatory measures that had long been used. That did not make them acceptable, but it did pose a problem as to what principle could be used to oppose them. Through all the period surrounding the War for Independence, there were men who used their minds and pens to formulate positions which would galvanize opinion. They were usually thoughtful men, not hot-headed revolutionaries. The man who came forward to perform this service of setting forth a position on the Townshend duties was John Dickinson.

Dickinson was born in Maryland, was sometimes from Pennsylvania, but was most often from Delaware, when the distinction was made. He belongs in that select circle of men entitled to be called Founding Fathers. From 1767 to 1775 he was the theoretician of colonial resistance.

Dickinson's position on the Townshend duties first appeared as separate letters published weekly in the *Pennsylvania Chronicle and Universal Advertiser*, a newspaper, beginning November 30, 1767. New England newspapers began publishing them in December, and before it was over all colonial newspapers, except four, published them. They were published as a pamphlet in 1768, went through seven American printings, plus one in Dublin, two in London, and a French translation.

## John Dickinson
## (1732-1808)

Dickinson was born in Maryland, educated in London, and lived most of his life in Pennsylvania and Delaware. He is sometimes called the "Penman of the Revolution", and was involved in most of the great political events from the Stamp Act Congress through the Constitutional Convention. He drafted the "Declaration of Rights" of the Stamp Act Congress, the "Olive Branch Petition", and the Articles of Confederation. Dickinson influenced Delaware to be the first to ratify the Constitution and Pennsylvania to move quickly to do so. He helped to found Dickinson College in 1783.

One historian sums up their impact this way: "Immediately, everyone took Dickinson's argument into account: Americans in assemblies, town meetings, and mass meetings adopted resolutions of thanks; British ministers wrung their hands; all the British press commented, and a portion of it applauded; malcontents read avidly; even the dilettantes of Paris salons discussed the Pennsylvania farmer."[83]

For one thing, the tone of the *Letters* was right. Dickinson not only claimed a formal loyalty to the king and the empire but actually cast his argument in terms of their well being. Though the natural law philosophy underlay much of what he wrote, he did not emphasize natural laws and rights so as to distinguish them in a divisive manner from the rights of Britons under the Constitution. His appeal was to tradition, precedent, prudence, self-interest (both of Britain and America), the desire for liberty, and continuity with the past. And though he bade Americans to resist the Townshend duties, he proposed that they do so in an orderly fashion. First, they should send petitions; if they did not get results, turn to something like a boycott of goods; only when all peaceful means had failed should other approaches be considered. But he pled with Americans not to give in to a spirit of riotousness. "The cause of *liberty* is a cause of too much dignity to be sullied by turbulence and tumult. It ought to be maintained in a manner suitable to her nature. Those who engage in it should breathe a sedate, yet fervent spirit, animating them to actions of prudence, justice, modesty, bravery, humanity and magnanimity."[84]

The great appeal of Dickinson's pamphlet stemmed from the fact that he tore the argument for the Townshend duties apart and left it in shreds. These duties were no better than the stamp tax, only more subtle. As for these duties being acceptable because they were external taxes, he thought the case hardly worth considering. The objection to taxation by Parliament was not based upon a distinction between external and internal; the only valid distinction was between taxation for the purpose of raising revenue and incidental levies for the regulation of trade. Americans accepted, he pointed out, as they had accepted, British regulation of American trade, but not taxation for revenue. The latter were clearly taxes, and they involved the taking of property without the consent of the owners. True, incidental revenues might arise from the regulation of trade, but they were a consequence, not the cause of it. No such case could be made for the Townshend duties; they were laid on items which must be bought from the British. Certainly, it was not the aim of the British to prohibit or restrain such trade. In fact, it was simply a tax, for the colonists were not permitted to obtain the goods elsewhere and might, if the British chose, be prohibited from manufacturing them.

But the main point was that the colonies were not represented in Parliament, that taxes take property, and that the more Parliament intruded in this way the less secure was property in America. "If the parliament have a right," Dickinson said, "to lay a duty of Four Shillings and Eight-pence on a hundred weight of glass, or a ream of paper, they have a right to lay a duty of any other sum on either.... If *they* have any right to tax *us*—then, whether *our own money* shall continue in *our own pockets* or not depends no longer on *us,* but on *them.*"[85]

Colonial legislatures began to act in 1768; Dickinson's arguments had struck home. Massachusetts took the lead in February by drawing up a Circular Letter which it send around to the other colonies. This letter was endorsed by New Hampshire, Virginia, Maryland, Connecticut, Rhode Island, Georgia and South Carolina, sometimes by the assemblies, and, if they were not in session, by the speaker of the house. The British reply came in April from the Earl of Hillborough; it was sent as a circular letter. He had already written to the governor of Massachusetts ordering him to have the house of representatives rescind their Circular Letter at the next session. To the other governors, he expressed his hope that their assemblies would not take part in this new effort to arouse resentment to British rule. "But if notwithstanding these expectations and your most earnest endeavors, there should appear in the Assembly of your Province a disposition to receive or give any Countenance to this seditious paper [the Massachusetts Circular Letter], it will be your duty to prevent any proceeding upon it" by dissolving or dismissing the assembly.[86] Since this obviously did not work, additional troops were ordered to Boston in June 1768.

On the other hand, it was becoming clear to the colonists from these and other instances—the harassment of shippers by customs agents, the

increasing of military forces in the colonies, the rejection of petitions—that petitions and resolutions alone would not produce a change
in British policy. The colonists, then, moved toward hitting Britain
where it would hurt—in trade. Boston took the lead in adopting a non-
importation agreement in August of 1768. What they proposed to do
was to stop almost all imports from Britain. The movement to do this
spread through the colonies, though it was rough going. Understand-
ably, importers and shippers were not enthusiastic about reducing imports, especially those for whom this was a major source of income.
Moreover, if non-importation was going to work it needed to be a concerted effort throughout the colonies. If it were not, ports which remained open to British goods could benefit at the expense of those
which closed their ports to them. The colonists did succeed in closing
down the major port cities to most British imports in the course of 1769.
The best weapon against ports which did not cooperate was to cut off
commercial relations with them. This usually brought them into line.

Though non-importation was far from absolute, it did succeed. Imports from Great Britain into the colonies fell from 2,157,218 pounds in
1768 to 1,336,122 in 1769. Some ports did much better than this
average. For example, Philadelphia's imports from Britain dropped
from 432,000 pounds in 1768 to 200,000 in 1769 to 135,000 in 1770.
More important, since the object of non-importation was not simply to
reduce imports from Britain, the British began to back down once more
in the face of colonial opposition. In 1769 Parliament moderated its
position on the Quartering Act. In 1770 Lord North became the head of
the British government, a position which he held until 1782. His government was at first conciliatory, and in April 1770 the Townshend duties
were repealed, except for the tax on tea.

It was not long before the non-importation agreements began to be
abandoned. There was considerable sentiment for continuing
them—after all, the tax on tea had not been repealed, nor had other
sources of tension been removed— but many of the merchants had had
enough of such self-denial. By various maneuvers, they opened up the
ports to British goods once again. This course was the more attractive
generally because the hasty efforts at increasing domestic manufactures
to replace British imports had produced little of consequence.

The colonies were comparatively calm during 1771. Although there
had been clashes between British troops and colonists at New York and
Boston in 1770 (the latter leading to the "Boston Massacre"), these did
not expand into any general conflict. What remained of the British
threat to the colonies was difficult to dramatize; there could hardly be
said to be a trend toward oppression if the oppressive measures were being reduced. At any rate, no major figure ventured forth to attempt a
dramatization. Even though tea continued to be taxed, the amount of

tea imported into the colonies by way of England increased from the low point for the past several years of 110,000 pounds in 1770 to 362,000 pounds in 1771. The quiet brought with it a return of prosperity, too.

## *The British Resolve to Use Force*

It was, however, the calm before the storm, the first clouds of which began to gather in 1772. It began when Rhode Islanders burned the British revenue ship, the *Gaspee*. The *Gaspee* had been harassing shipping coming into Rhode Island for some time; the captain was particularly obnoxious in his treatment of those on ships stopped for searches. The *Gaspee* ran aground and while she was in that disabled condition, a party boarded her, drove the crew off and burned the ship. An investigating committee turned up no useful information, but its appointment from England stirred resentment. A little later in the year, the British exchequer took over the payment of the salaries of the governor and judges in Massachusetts. Here was the move that had long been sought: to remove crown officials from reliance on the elected legislature. In November Boston formed a Committee of Correspondence which sent statements to other towns in Massachusetts and to all colonial assemblies. Early the next year the House of Burgesses in Virginia established a Committee of Correspondence, and most other colonies followed suit.

What stirred the colonists to open resistance once again, however, was the Tea Act in May 1773. This new act was not intended to aggravate the situation in the colonies. Actually, tea from British shippers would be less expensive than formerly. The British hoped to rescue the East India Company, which was having great difficulty disposing of its tea in competition with the Dutch. While the Dutch were not permitted to sell tea in the British American colonies, it was being acquired by smugglers and sold here. By the Tea Act Parliament intended to undercut this illegal trade. The East India Company was permitted to sell tea directly to the colonies rather than having to sell it at auction first in England, as it had done theretofore. In this way, tea could be sold at a lower price in the colonies than in England.

The British were about to be able to do what John Dickinson had indicated to be the danger. They were going to establish a monopoly for a taxed item, something which could not be competitively produced in America, but was very popular. It is likely that had Parliament contented itself with nailing down what was already supposed to be a monopoly it might have got away with it. But the fact that tea was taxed entangled the monopoly question with taxation-without-representation. The objections that had been raised before now had a fresh example,

## Samuel Adams
## (1722-1803)

Adams was born in Boston, educated at Harvard, and went into his father's brewery business. His greatest fame was won as a patriot leader up to the time of the War for Independence. He helped to organize the Sons of Liberty, started the Committee of Correspondence, and probably joined with John Hancock in organizing the Boston Tea Party. He worked to arouse opposition to the Sugar, Stamp and Townshend Acts, served in the Massachusetts House of Representatives, the Continental Congress and as governor of his state.

but now Americans were to be seduced into compliance by a lower price.

It did not happen. True, the East India Company caused chests of tea to be loaded on many ships for America, and these put into port at such places as Boston, New York and Charleston. In most places the tea was never landed. At New York the Sons of Liberty took the lead in preventing its unloading. At Boston, for fear that the tea would be seized by customs officials and somehow sold, Bostonians disguised themselves rather poorly as Mohawk Indians and dumped the tea in the harbor. Patriots prevented the tea from being landed at Philadelphia. It was landed and transferred to the customs house at Charleston; there it stayed until war came. Beyond that, such a vigorous campaign was carried out against the drinking of tea that coffee replaced it as a hot beverage for Americans, and hot tea has ever since been suspect in America.

This time Parliament did not back down when confronted by colonial resistance. Heretofore the British had been conciliatory, yielding in practice, if not theory, to colonial pressure. But now there was mounting determination in Parliament to use force, if need be, on the colonists. Certainly Boston must be punished, and the whole colony of Massachusetts brought to heel. Between March 31 and June 2, 1774, Parliament passed four bills which are known collectively as the Coercive Acts. The Boston Port Act closed the port of Boston until such time as the East India Company had been compensated for its tea. The Massachusetts Government Act provided (1) that the governor's council would be appointed by the king, not elected as had been the case, (2) that the governor and king would appoint judges, (3) that juries would be chosen by the sheriff, and (4) that town meetings could not be held without the consent of the governor, except for annual election meetings. In short, citizens of Massachusetts were to lose control over much of their government. The two other acts applied to all the colonies. The Administration of Justice Act provided for the trying of key colonial officials in England, if the government thought it desirable. The Quartering Act authorized the quartering of troops in occupied dwellings.

The colonists dubbed them the Intolerable Acts.

The issue was joined, and unremittingly pressed after Parliament passed the Coercive Acts in 1774. George III declared in September of that year that "the die is now cast, the colonies must either submit or triumph...."[87] Young Alexander Hamilton described the situation this way: "What then is the subject of our controversy with the mother country?—It is this; whether we shall preserve that security to our lives and properties, which the law of nature, the genius of the British Constitution, and our charters afford us; or whether we shall resign them into the hands of the British House of Commons...."[88] Faced with the British determination to compel their submission, the colonists were being driven to the point where only one question would remain. Independence or submission?

# Notes

1. Frederic Harrison, *The Meaning of History and Other Historical Pieces* (New York, 1914), p. 5, as quoted in Henry S. Commager, *The Study of History* (Columbus, Ohio: Charles E. Merrill, 1966), pp. 2-3.

2. A.G. Dickens, *Reformation and Society in Sixteenth Century Europe* (New York: Harcourt, Brace and World, 1966), p. 156.

3. Wallace K. Ferguson, *Europe in Transition* (Boston: Houghton Mifflin, 1962), p. 413.

4. G.M. Trevelyan, *History of England*, vol. II (New York: Doubleday, 1952), p. 100.

5. Wallace Notestein, *The English People on the Eve of Colonization* (New York: Harper & Row, 1954), p. 36.

6. *Ibid.*, p. 46.

7. Christopher Hill, *The Century of Revolution* (New York: W.W. Norton, 1961), pp. 75-76.

8. *Ibid.*, pp. 28-29.

9. Trevelyan, *op. cit.*, p. 135.

10. Ralph Linton, *The Tree of Culture* (New York: Alfred A. Knopf, 1955), p. 591.

11. Samuel E. Morison, *The Oxford History of the American People* (New York: Oxford University Press, 1965), p. 14.

12. *Encyclopedia Britannica* (1955 edition), vol. XIV, p. 696.

13. Max Savelle and Robert Middlekauff, *A History of Colonial America* (New York: Holt, Rinehart and Winston, 1964), p. 86.

14. Quoted in Lyon G. Tyler, *England in America*, 1580-1652 (New York: Greenwood Press, 1969), pp. 73-74.

15. Curtis P. Nettels, *The Roots of American Civilization* (New York: Appleton-Century-Crofts, 1963, 2nd ed.), p. 223.

16. Harvey Wish, *The American Historian* (New York: Oxford University Press, 1960), p. 3.

17. Quoted in Herbert L. Osgood, *The American Colonies in the Seventeenth Century*, vol. I (Gloucester, Mass.: Peter Smith, 1957), p. 153.

18. Savelle and Middlekauff, *op. cit.*, pp. 152-54.

19. Clinton Rossiter, *The First American Revolution* (New York: Harcourt, Brace and Co., A Harvest Book, 1956), p. 19.

20. Nelson M. Blake, *A History of American Life and Thought* (New York: McGraw-Hill, 1963), p. 17.

21. Francis B. Simkins, *A History of the South* (New York: Alfred A. Knopf, 1953), p. 64.

22. Clarence L. ver Steeg, *The Formative Years*, 1607-1763 (New York: Hill and Wang, 1964), p. 193.

23. Osgood, *op. cit.*, p. 424.

24. Daniel J. Boorstin, *The Americans: The Colonial Experience* (New York: Vintage Books, 1958), p. 106.

25. Eliot's *Debates*, Bk. I, vol. 3, pp. 294-95.

26. *Ibid.*, vol. 2, p. 278.

27. Boorstin, *op. cit.*, p. 105.

28. *Ibid.*, p. 99.

29. Quoted in W.T. Jones, *A History of Western Philosophy* (New York: Harcourt, Brace and Co., 1952), pp. 656-57.

30. Robert Lekachman, *A History of Economic Ideas* (New York: Harper & Row, 1959), pp. 45-46.

31. Nettels, *op. cit.*, p. 283.

32. Gilbert C. Fite and Jim E. Reese, *An Economic History of the United States* (Boston: Houghton Mifflin, 1965, 2nd ed.), p . 53.

33. E.A.J. Johnson, *American Economic Thought in the Seventeenth Century* (New York: Russell and Russell, 1961), p. 29.

34. *Ibid.*, p. 254.

35. Fite and Reese, *op. cit.*, pp. 67-68.

36. Eugen Weber, *A Modern History of Europe* (New York: W.W. Norton, 1971), pp. 145-46.

37. W.E. Lunt, *History of England* (New York: Harper & Bros., 1956), p. 470.

38. Lawrence H. Gipson, *The Coming of the Revolution* (New York: Harper Torchbooks, 1962), p. 58.

39. Quoted in John C. Miller, *Origins of the American Revolution* (Boston: Little, Brown and Co., 1943), p. 8.

40. Nettels, *op. cit.*, p. 252.

41. Quoted in Blake, *op. cit.*, p. 56.

42. Louis B. Wright, *The Cultural Life of the American Colonies,* 1607-1763 (New York: Harper & Row, 1957), p. 130.

43. *Ibid.*, p. 138.

44. Merle Curti, *The Growth of American Thought* (New York: Harper & Bros., 1951, 2nd ed.), p. 83.

45. Quoted in Robert E. Spiller, *et al.*, eds., *Literary History of the United States* (New York: Macmillan, 1953, rev. ed.), p . 40.

46. Quoted in *ibid.*, p. 46.

47. Perry Miller, ed., *The American Puritans* (Garden City, N.Y.: Doubleday Anchor Books, 1956), p. 310.

48. Spiller, *op. cit.*, p . 80.

49. Quoted in Stow Persons, *American Minds* (New York: Henry Holt and Co., 1958), p. 71.

50. George A. Peek, Jr., ed., *The Political Writings of John Adams* (New York: Liberal Arts Press, 1954), p . 96.

51. Weber, *op. cit.*, p . 358.

52. Wilson O. Clough, ed., *Intellectual Origins of American National Thought* (New York: Corinth Books, 1961, 2nd ed.), p . 149.

53. Eugen Weber, ed., *The Western Tradition* (Boston: D.C. Heath, 1959), p. 425.

54. *Ibid.*

55. Clough, *op. cit.*, p. 153.

56. David L. Jacobson, ed., *The English Libertarians* (Indianapolis: Bobbs-Merrill, 1965), p. 108.

57. *Ibid.*, p. xxxvi.

58. *Ibid.*, p . 38.

59. *Ibid.*, p. 70.

60. Nettels, *op. cit.*, p. 546.

61. Jack P. Greene, "The Role of the Lower Houses of Assembly in Eighteenth Century Politics," *Essays in American Colonial History*, Paul Goodman, ed. (New York: Holt, Rinehart and Winston, 1967), pp. 431-32.

62. Nettels, *op. cit.*, p. 563.

63. Quoted in Boorstin, *op. cit.*, p. 127.

64. T.S. Ashton, *An Economic History of England: The Eighteenth Century* (London: Metheun, 1955), p. 130.

65. Christopher Hill, *The Century of Revolution* (New York: W.W. Norton, 1966), pp. 263-64.

66. Preserved Smith, *The Enlightenment*, 1687-1776 (New York: Collier Books, 1962, originally pub. 1934), p. 194.

67. Adam Smith, *The Wealth of Nations,* Edwin Canaan, ed. (New Rochelle, N.Y.: Arlington House, n.d.), vol. II, p. 27.

68. John Braeman, ed., *The Road to Independence* (New York: Capricorn Books, 1963), pp. 13-14.

69. Jack P. Greene, ed., *Colonies to Nation* (New York: McGraw-Hill, 1967), pp. 17-18.

70. Braeman, *op. cit.*, pp. 17-19.

71. Greene, *Colonies to Nation, op. cit.*, p. 44.

72. *Ibid.*, p. 24.

73. *Ibid.*, p. 44.

74. Quoted in Merrill Jensen, *The Founding of a Nation* (New York: Oxford University Press, 1968), pp . 63-64.

75. Quoted in Gipson, *op. cit.*, p. 87.

76. Quoted in Richard B. Morris, *The American Revolution* (Princeton: D. Van Nostrand, 1955), p. 90.

77. *Ibid.*, p. 91.

78. Jensen, *op. cit.*, p . 86.

79. Quoted in Gipson, *op. cit.*, p. 105.

80. Greene, *Colonies to Nation, op. cit.*, p. 85.

81. Quoted in Edmund S. Morgan, "Colonial Ideas of Parliamentary Power," *The Reinterpretation of the American Revolution*, Jack P. Greene, ed. (New York: Harper & Row, 1968), p. 166.

82. Greene, *Colonies to Nation, op. cit.*, pp. 88-89.

83. Forrest McDonald, intro., *Empire and Nation* ( Englewood Cliffs, N.J.: Prentice-Hall, 1962), p. xiii.

84. *Ibid.*, p. 17.

85. *Ibid.*, pp. 43-44.

86. Greene, *Colonies to Nation, op. cit.*, p. 143.

87. Quoted in Jensen, *op. cit.*, p. 572.

88. Leslie F.S. Upton, ed., *Revolutionary versus Loyalist* (Waltham, Mass.: Blaisdell, 1968), p. 21.

# Glossary

**Admiralty, the**—the department in Britain in charge of naval affairs. During the colonial period it was much involved in regulating colonial trade, and protecting it at sea.

**Chattel slavery**—a condition in which a person is owned as the property of another. Chattels are a species of property, namely, *movable* property. Since Negro slaves were movable property in America, their status was described as chattel slavery.

**Church of England**—the church established in England after it was withdrawn from the Roman Catholic Church. It was also established in some of the colonies. It is also called the Anglican Church. The Episcopal Church in the United States is a descendant of the Church of England.

**Civilization**—usually refers to the shared outlook, beliefs and manner of conducting their affairs that generally make for civility and peace among peoples over a broad geographical area. It should be distinguished from a culture, which may be a particular application of a civilization in a country or among a people.

**Classical**—an adjective which describes something modeled after the earliest and highest examples of it. In history it most often refers to art and literature modeled after that of the great ages of Greece and Rome, or Classical Antiquity. It also connotes a style of order, balance and harmony of expression.

**Empire**—a political territory made up of peoples of different backgrounds, languages and traditions, but all under one central government. It may contain within its bounds several distinct nations or states, each with their own local governments. Examples would be the Roman Empire, the Ottoman Empire and the British Empire.

**Established Church**—a church which is supported by the government. The clergy may be paid from taxes, attendance at the services required, and the rules of the church enforced by law. The church may also be given a religious monopoly, i.e., be the only church permitted.

**Exports**—goods shipped out of one country to another, as, for example, Americans export grain to Japan.

**Government intervention**—describes government action to regulate or control what would otherwise be voluntary peaceful activities. It is most often used to refer to interference in the economy, but it can refer as well to religion or any other area of human activity. Mercantile regulations were government intervention.

**Hellenistic civilization**—that civilization built around Greek influence which spread around the Mediterranean in the wake of the conquests of Alexander the Great.

**Hierarchy**—a system of rule or control by graded ranks of rulers, as emperors, kings, dukes, earls, etc., or in religion of archbishops, bishops, abbotts and the like.

**High Middle Ages**—the 12th and 13th centuries when medieval civilization reached the peak of its development.

**Humanism**—arose as a term to describe artistic and literary developments during the Renaissance. It refers especially to the Renaissance interest in and imitation of the individualistic, humane and, possibly, Pagan aspects of the ancient Greeks and Romans. It was not anti-Christian, usually, and the outlook which came out of it most often can be described as Christian Humanism. In any case, Renaissance humanism was different from contemporary humanism, which is atheistic and focuses exclusively on the human and earthly aspects of reality.

**Imports**—goods brought into a country from other countries, as for example, Americans import coffee from Brazil.

**Indentured servant**—a person bound for a specific length of time, usually 4 to 7 years, of servitude to a master. The master had contractual rights to the services of the servant for several years; after which, the servant could be free if he chose. Many Europeans came to America as indentured servants.

**Islam**—means surrender (to the will of Allah). It consists of the body of believers in the religion taught by Mohammed. They are commonly called Moslems.

**Medieval**—refers to the period in European history between the fall of Rome (476 A.D.) and the Italian Renaissance (circa 1450). It is a synonym for Middle Ages. It refers also to the style, character or ways of viewing, organizing and doing things during that period.

**Mercantilism**—an economic system in which the economy is regulated, directed and controlled for nationalist ends. It comprehends, too, the idea that a nation's wealth consists of its holdings of precious metals.

**Modern**—used in history to refer to the time from the Renaissance to the present. The word is used with many other significations, as for example, modern art, which refers to a style of painting that has emerged in the past hundred years or so. More loosely still, the latest design of some device—automobile, typewriter, stove or what not—may be called modern. However, in the history of civilization, it has a much broader meaning and comprehends a whole range of developments.

**Monarchy**—means, literally, rule by one. Thus a king, queen or emperor may be a monarch. Monarchy is usually based on heredity, and descent to the throne follows rules to determine that the monarch holds power legitimately. This is one way it can be clearly distinguished from contemporary dictatorships, which are usually based on personal seizure of power.

**Natural law**—refers to the laws of nature, whether they be laws governing the behavior of physical objects, laws of development, laws flowing from human nature and man's situation on earth, or those that are congenial to constructive accomplishments among men.

**Natural rights**—rights arising from the nature of man and the conditions of individual and social life on earth. They are also said to be God-given, not owing their rightfulness to government or any other human institution.

**Parliament**—is composed, in Britain, of a House of Commons and a House of Lords. The members of Commons are elected to represent districts. The Lords temporal, those whose power stems from wordly possessions, usually inherit their positions. The Lords spiritual are appointed to their high positions in the Church of England.

**Patent**—an exclusive right or privilege (monopoly) over the use or disposal of something. Patents were usually issued by the king at the time of the settlement of America, and they might be for anything ranging from the right to sell in some market to control or ownership of land. Charters, deeds, copyrights and patents for inventions are descendants of such patents.

**Plantation**—usually meant, in the colonial period, what we might call a settlement or community. Sometimes it might refer to a colony. In any case, the distinction between plantation and colony was not carefully made. In the course of time, the lands and dwellings belonging to Southern planters came to be called plantations. Thus the word acquired a specialized meaning.

**Property**—is either fixed or movable. Fixed property consists of land and any buildings upon it, and is called *real* property, or real estate. Movable property is called chattels, and consists of anything that is not attached to the land. The produce of property, as a general rule, belongs to the property owner.

**Puritan**—an English term to refer to those whose religious faith derives from Calvinism. The word specifically calls attention to their desire to purify the church. The settlers of New England were most apt to be Puritans. The two denominations with closest links to this movement are Congregationalists and Presbyterians.

**Quartering**—military personnel reside in *quarters*, i.e., rooms, housing, tents or buildings. Quartering has to do with providing such facilities. Thus a quartering act requires somebody to provide quarters for troops.

**Revenue**—the income of government, usually arising from taxes, though it may come from such varied sources as licenses, fees, the sale of land, charges for services, tariffs or others.

**Staple crops**—the principal crop or crops grown in a region for sale on the market, primarily in foreign trade. For example, tobacco, rice and indigo were staple crops in the American colonies.

**Tariff**—charges placed on goods by government that are shipped into or out of a country. Rates are placed on particular commodities and may vary as to their percentage of the selling price from one commodity to another. Tariffs are also referred to as duties and customs charges.

**Whigs**—the members of one of the first political parties in England. Their special appeal was to merchants, shippers, manufacturers and townsmen, and they usually promoted foreign trade and colonial development.

# Suggestions for
# Additional Reading

There is a vast literature on American colonial history and the European background to it. It ranges from books covering the whole period to monographs on aspects of the history to biographies of individuals to multivolumed works dealing with particular colonies. What follows then, is only a brief selection from among these which is meant more to suggest the range of material available than the scope of research and writing that has gone on. Since the focus of this work is on the transplantation of European civilization and its continuation in America, many of the selections will either have that emphasis or contribute in some way to understanding it.

Of general histories of the United States, Samuel E. Morison's *Oxford History of the American People* covers the colonial period with more than the usual thoroughness, though he does not go much into the European background. Two textbooks on the colonial period are Max Savelle and Robert Middlekauff, *A History of Colonial America* and Curtis Nettels, *The Roots of American Civilization*. Among the general works on the colonial period that cover it in much detail are: Herbert L. Osgood, *American Colonies in the Seventeenth Century* (3 volumes) and *American Colonies in the Eighteenth Century;* Charles M. Andrews, *The Colonial Period in American History*; Lawrence H. Gipson, *The British Empire before the American Revolution* (many volumes); and George L. Beer, *The Old Colonial System.* The older works by Francis Parkman and John Fiske are still of interest and make good reading. Parkman's account of the Battle of Quebec at the conclusion of the French and Indian War is an enduring masterpiece.

Those who are interested in the European background before the time of Columbus may wish to begin with the ancient Greeks and Romans. Excellent introductions to these peoples can be found in *The Greek Way* and *The Roman Way*. H.D.F. Kitto's *The Greeks*, in a Pelican edition, provides much valuable information on its subject. A discerning older study of the institutions of both Greece and Rome is Fustel De Coulanges, *The Ancient City.* Taylor Caldwell's *A Pillar of Iron* provides a vibrant fictional account of the world of Cicero and the last years of the Roman Republic. For the Middle Ages, good introductions can be found in Robert S. Hoyt, *Europe in the Middle Ages* and James W. Thompson and Edgar N. Johnson, *An Introduction to Medieval Europe*. Frederick B. Artz, *The Mind of the Middle Ages*, provides many insights into the outlook, art and culture of that era. At a more general level, Russell Kirk has explored the whole framework of the European background and applied it to the founding of the United States in *The Roots of American Order.*

The transition from the Medieval to the modern is told in Wallace K. Ferguson, *Europe in Transition, 1300-1520.* E.P. Cheyney's *Dawn of a New Era* carries the story into the new age. Henry S. Lucas, *The Renaissance and the Reformation* provides thorough coverage of these subjects. Among older works, Jacob Burckhardt's *The Civilization of the Renaissance in Italy* is a valuable study. Will Durant, *The Renaissance,* provides a readable account. Albert Hyma has told the story of *The Christian Renaissance.* Preserved Smith, *The Age of the Reformation,* gives an overview earlier account, and a more recent one is in H.J. Grimm, *The Reformation Era.* A general work on "The Great Age of Discovery from Columbus to the Present" is Joachim G. Leithauser, *Worlds Beyond the Horizon.* John B. Brebner, *The Explorer's of North America,* is a standard work on the subject. Samuel E. Morison's *Admiral of the Ocean Sea* describes the several voyages of Columbus. Lawrence B. Packard, *The Commercial Revolution* tells the story of the expansion of European trade in the wake of the discoveries of the 15th and 16th centuries.

An important work on the English background is Wallace Notestein, *The English People on the Eve of Colonization.* Other valuable works on the English of this period are: G.J. Trevelyan, *History of England,* vol. II, *The Tudors and the Stuart Era*; Christopher Hill, *The Century of Revolution*; William C.H. Wood, *Elizabethan Sea-Dogs*; Alfred L. Rouse, *The Elizabethans and America.* For the American Indians, see Clark Wissler, *The Indians of the United States: Four Centuries of Their History and Culture*; Roy H. Pearce, *The Savages of America: A Study of the Indian and the Idea of Civilization*; John Collier, *The Indians of the Americas*; Harold Driver, *The Indians of North America.*

For the settlement and development of the colonies, the following suggests the sorts of topics that have been explored: Wesley F. Craven, *The Southern Colonies in the Seventeenth Century*; Thomas J. Wertenbaker, *Virginia Under the Stuarts,* 1607-1688; Louis B. Wright, *The First Gentlemen of Virginia*; Matthew P. Andrews, *The Founding of Maryland*; James T. Adams, *The Founding of New England*; Samuel E. Morison, *Builders of the Bay Colony*; Perry Miller, ed., *The American Puritans*; D.W. Connor, *Studies in the History of North Carolina*; Edward McGrady, *The History of South Carolina under the Proprietary Government*; Verner W. Crane, *The Southern Frontier*; Ellis H. Roberts, *New York* (2 volumes); Edwin P. Tanner, *The Province of New Jersey*; William C. Braithwaite, *The Beginnings of Quakerism*; Edwin B. Bronner, *William Penn's "Holy Experiment," The Founding of Pennsylvania*; Ola E. Winslow, *Jonathan Edwards*; William H. Fry, *New Hampshire as a Royal Province*; Richmond C. Beatty, *William Byrd of Westover*; Robert Wright, *A Memoir of General Oglethorpe;* James T. Adams, *Colonial Society;* Clinton Rossiter, *Seed-Time of the Republic;* Curtis P. Nettels, *The Money Supply in the American Colonies*; Arthur C. Bining, *British Regulation of the Colonial Iron Industry*; Michael Kraus, *The Atlantic Civilization*; Wesley M. Gewehr, *The Great Awakening in Virginia*; William W. Sweet, *Religion in Colonial America*; Max Savelle, *Seeds of Liberty*; Whitfield J. Bell, *Early American Science.*

# INDEX